The Intuitive Spark

OTHER HAY HOUSE TITLES BY SONIA CHOQUETTE

Books and Card Decks

The Answer Is Simple (available August 2008)

Ask Your Guides

Ask Your Guides Oracle Cards

Diary of a Psychic

Divine Guidance Oracle Cards (available October 2008)

The Time Has Come . . . (available April 2008)

Soul Lessons and Soul Purpose

Soul Lessons and Soul Purpose Oracle Cards

Trust Your Vibes

Trust Your Vibes at Work, and Let Them Work for <u>You</u>

Trust Your Vibes Oracle Cards

Vitamins for the Soul

CD Programs

Attunement to Higher Vibrational Living (4-CD set),
with Mark Stanton Welch

How to Trust Your Vibes at Work and Let Them Work for <u>You</u>
(4-CD set)

Meditations for Receiving Divine Guidance (2-CD set)

Trust Your Vibes (6-CD set)

Please visit:

Hay House USA: **www.hayhouse.com**®
Hay House Australia: **www.hayhouse.com.au**
Hay House UK: **www.hayhouse.co.uk**
Hay House South Africa: **www.hayhouse.co.za**
Hay House India: **www.hayhouse.co.in**

The Intuitive Spark

Bringing Intuition Home to
Your Child, Your Family, and You

Sonia Choquette

HAY HOUSE, INC.
Carlsbad, California • New York City
London • Sydney • Johannesburg
Vancouver • Hong Kong • New Delhi

Published and distributed in the United States by: Hay House, Inc.: www.hayhouse. com • *Published and distributed in Australia by:* Hay House Australia Pty. Ltd.: www. hayhouse.com.au • *Published and distributed in the United Kingdom by:* Hay House UK, Ltd.: www.hayhouse.co.uk • *Published and distributed in the Republic of South Africa by:* Hay House SA (Pty), Ltd.: www.hayhouse.co.za • *Distributed in Canada by:* Raincoast: www.raincoast.com • *Published in India by:* Hay House Publishers India: www.hayhouse.co.in

Editorial supervision: Jill Kramer • *Design:* Tricia Breidenthal

Originally published under the title *The Wise Child,* © 1999, by Three Rivers Press, a registered trademark of Random House, Inc. ISBN: 0-609-80399-9

Library of Congress Cataloging-in-Publication Data

Choquette, Sonia.
  [Wise child]
  The intuitive spark : bringing intuition home to your child, your family, and you / Sonia Choquette.
    p. cm.
  Originally published: Wise child. 1st ed. New York : Three Rivers Press, c1999.
  ISBN-13: 978-1-4019-1738-8 (tradepaper) 1. Intuition. 2. Child rearing. I. Title.
  BF315.5.C48 2007
  153.4'4--dc22   2007008189

ISBN: 978-1-4019-1738-8

10 09 08 07   5 4 3 2
1st edition, November 2007
2nd edition, November 2007

Printed in the United States of America

This book is dedicated to my daughters,
Sonia and Sabrina,
who are my inspiration;
and to my mother,
who fully empowered me.

Contents

Author's note: The names of many of the people in this book have been changed to protect the privacy of my clients.

Introduction

In My House

I live in a large, sunny home on a tree-lined street in Chicago. I share the house with my husband, Patrick; my two daughters, Sonia and Sabrina; our dog, Miss T; and a steady stream of clients who come to see me in my role as intuitive guide and counselor. Every day I sit in my office, amid my books and spiritual talismans, and listen to people ask about their deepest dreams and desires. Often I feel that the room is crowded with far more than the presence of my client and me—entire families seem to stand in the wings, because many individuals' dearest dreams are related to the well-being and happiness of those they love.

"How can I help my children thrive and prosper?" I'm often asked. "How can I teach them to trust themselves so that they won't become unhappy or frustrated like I've been? How can I protect them and give them the tools they need to be the best they can?"

"Kids learn from what we do," I tell my clients gently. "If you want them to thrive as joyful and well-integrated beings, you must show them how. You need to create an environment in your home that honors their fullest flowering. You have to recognize that they, like you, are spiritual beings; and as such, they have a direct connection to the loving Source of all wisdom. This link is experienced as a 'sixth sense,' their intuition. You must develop and honor their inner knowing if you're to raise what I call fully empowered and happy children."

"But Sonia, how do I do that?"

"Step-by-step," I answer. "You must awaken in them a sense of their soulful heritage; and provide an atmosphere of spiritual safety, support, and well-being. You begin to do this by first creating that sacred awareness within *yourself*. As a parent, you set the tone for their intuitive awakening. You're the source from which your children take their cues. A spiritually conscious and integrated dad or mom who has a strong connection to his or her own inner guidance and well-being makes it possible for that same quality to flourish in kids and at home."

"But Sonia, that sounds impossible to me! How did you learn to be so tuned in to your intuition? How did you come to recognize and embrace your sixth sense so completely, and then instill this deep-seated wisdom in your family?"

People wonder if I was born with a special gift or had some mystical experience at an early age—whether it's simply a case of "either you've got it or you don't."

"We're all attuned to Divine wisdom because we're all spiritual beings," I tell my clients. "Intuition is our heart-based connection to our Inner Teacher, the guiding voice of our Higher Self. The difference is that I was brought up knowing this. In my case—and I believe in many instances where a person has a strong and useful innate awareness—the most significant and influential factor in my development was the mother I had, as well as a family environment that not only allowed for this ability but actually *centered* on and respected it."

Let me take a moment to tell you about my own mom.

My Mother's Story

My mom, the Sonia for whom I was named, was born in Romania to an artistic and religious mother, and a sensual and passionate father. The second youngest of ten children, she lived a life of comfort and privilege in a country setting where her dad produced wine. My mother recalls that both her parents had a very strong spiritual awareness and an active sense of intuition. My grandmother, a devout woman, prayed openly for Divine guidance and freely acknowledged the constant flow of inner direction she received in all matters. Her relationship to God and the Universe made her feel loved and protected, and she passed this sense of well-being on to her children. My grandfather, a practical man, would wheel and deal with the townspeople, making decisions according to his gut instincts. His hunches were reliable—a fact he celebrated unabashedly—and the family prospered. Through her parents, my mother learned that inner guidance was available for the asking and that following its lead was the best way to direct her life. Her connection to her spirit's wisdom was organic and intimate, and it became second nature for her.

But my mom's idyllic life abruptly changed in the fall of 1943 when she was 12 years old. War had broken out in Europe, and one day she and her entire family, along with thousands of others in her town, were evacuated from their homes during an air raid. In the confusion, my mother was accidentally separated from her family. She was lucky to survive the bombing, but along with hundreds of other refugees, she was driven from the fields and rounded up as a prisoner. She and the others were forced to march for 11 days and nights into Germany, where they were put into a POW camp.

My mom told me that at this time of danger and crisis, when she was completely cut off from her family and safety, she found herself faced with the decision of either looking outward into a sea of terror, or turning inward for direction. For her, the choice was automatic. She did what she'd seen her parents do in a million subtle ways. With nothing outside herself to grasp on to, she looked within for help and found that her sixth sense kicked in with full force.

In my mother's case, intuition became her lifeline to survival. Without anyone to care for or protect her, and in the most extreme conditions of war, her inner voice consoled, grounded, and ultimately liberated her. While people around her were in despair and dying, something inside her fought back. An internal compass kept her focused on living. Its vigilant counsel was: "Look. Listen. Be aware! Stay calm!" Whenever she feared death, it would assure her: "No, not now. Not you." My mother said that it might just have been her fierce desire to survive, but her Divine awareness became her constant and beloved companion. And somehow, through its guidance, she always did manage to escape—often narrowly—mass executions, starvation, and even death by loss of hope.

The spring my mother was 14, soldiers in her camp began separating the prisoners; and she was shunted off with those to be sent to Odessa (in present-day Ukraine), where she knew that women were raped, tortured, and left to die. Panic welled up in her, but almost instantly it was quelled by the assurance of her inner voice once again saying, "No. Not this either." But in spite of her intuition, she was put on the Odessa train along with several hundred other captives.

As the train was pulling out of the station and gathering speed, my mom found herself in front of an open boxcar door. No one seemed to notice her. Like a shot her intuition shouted, "Now! Jump!" and the intensity of it *pushed* her outside. She leapt into the air, thinking that even death by falling would be less painful than what awaited her in Odessa.

Before she could even complete her thought, however, she hit the ground and rolled safely to a stop in a grassy field. She lay there for hours without moving before she dared to even test her arms and legs. Amazingly, not a bone was broken. Once again her inner counsel had saved her.

She stayed in the field for several days, but finally, weak with hunger and fatigue, she walked into a nearby village and turned herself in to the local townspeople. Initially, a farmer's wife took pity on her and hid her in a barn, offering her what little food was available. But as my mother later said, in many ways the villagers, too, were prisoners of the insanity of war; and eventually the family, fearing repercussions for harboring my mom, took her back to the military authorities of the prison camp.

By this time, however, the soldiers seemed less interested in dealing with her, and instead were only annoyed by this nuisance in the face of much larger problems. They put her in the kitchen of the Nazi general's headquarters and told her to help the cook. It was a miracle. She was safe and sound, and occasionally even managed to get a bit more than gruel for supper. Even so, she only weighed about 60 pounds.

A year and a half later, the tide of war turned. Suddenly the Americans descended upon the town, took over the headquarters, and liberated thousands of prisoners from the camps. My mother found herself on her own in the small Bavarian village of Dingolfing, living above a stable with a young Hungarian girl who had also just been freed. The name of the game at that point was survival of the fittest. My mom's sixth sense gave her a new and urgent directive: "Find food!"

Her remarkable spirit accepted the challenge, and the hunt was on. She learned to collect cigarette butts and reroll them to create new cigarettes, two of which could be traded for a single egg or potato. She also figured out how to gather wood, milk cows, sew, do needlepoint, and scrub dishes—whatever it took to scrape together a morsel of this or that. She wore cast-off army boots and an old sweater, and she wrapped rags around her legs to keep warm. As she later told me, "It was a time when we had the very best incentive to be creative."

Even after the liberation, despair prevailed among the survivors who found themselves displaced from home, separated from their families, without resources, and with no one in war-ravaged Germany to help them. But my mother didn't lose hope. With her intuition always cheering her on, she felt certain that she'd be all right.

"Perhaps it was youth, innocence, and naïveté," she says, "and perhaps it was denial on a monumental level, but never once would my inner guidance let me think about what could happen to me. It just urged me on, assuring me all the while to keep going, day by day."

The liberating American soldiers set up temporary law and order in the towns and villages of Germany; and in the fall of 1945, a young, handsome American soldier named Paul arrived in Dingolfing. All the girls admired him because he was so good-looking, and of course because he was in charge of the local base and known in town as "the Big Cheese." Once again my mom's inner voice had something to say about things. "He's the one for you," it declared, and she agreed.

One day she told her girlfriend about her intuition regarding Paul. The friend laughed out loud and said, "Sonia, the war must have scrambled your senses. Have you seen yourself lately? With so many blonde German girls in clean, beautiful clothes, all dying to meet him, why would he ever give somebody like you the time of day? I admire your optimism, but surely you're going too far!"

This angered my mother, and for the first time since her whole ordeal had begun, she started to doubt her sixth sense, which disturbed her considerably. After all, this guidance was all she had to keep herself alive. She retorted, "You're wrong! I *am* somebody! And my intuition is correct." Then she walked away, shaken and depressed.

As time passed, my mom continued to admire the handsome sergeant who sped around the town and countryside in his jeep. But he never once looked up and noticed her. Perhaps her friend was right, she thought. Maybe her inner voice was betraying her.

One spring day she was walking back to the village carrying two loads of firewood to the local guesthouse to exchange for a bowl of soup, when she noticed the soldier's jeep approaching at a fast clip. She stopped to watch him and gave him her biggest smile. He ignored her and barreled past, driving through a huge mud puddle and drenching her from head to toe. She was furious. What an insult!

She dropped her bundle and ran after his vehicle, yelling with fury. He must have heard or sensed her, because he looked into his rearview mirror and saw her covered with mud, waving her arms and screaming in a strange language. He stopped and drove back to apologize and help her; and the following year the dashing young Sergeant Paul Choquette married 16-year-old Sonia and brought her to America, where they settled in Denver and raised seven children. I was the second daughter to come along, and was named after my spunky mother.

Eventually my mom's family was found, and 20 years and a lifetime of experiences later, she was finally able to reunite with them.

When we were growing up, my mother gave us the best she had—the best her parents had instilled in her. She didn't have much formal education at the time, but she did have inner wisdom, and that treasure became the heartbeat of our family. She passed on the message that no matter what we faced in life—whatever the challenges or obstacles—if we turned inward to our hearts instead of allowing appearances to overwhelm us, and if we recognized and focused on our deep spiritual connection to the Universe, to God, then we would always be guided and protected, because that's the natural plan. The Universe would unquestionably show us what to do, where to go, and how to thrive, as it had done for her.

Our family's code word for this inner compass was *vibes*, because that's what intuition felt like—a subtle, vibrating energy that centered in the heart and moved outward to the gut, the chest, and the throat. Like waves of direction that were getting our attention as if to say, "Do this," "Go there," and "Avoid that," vibes ruled our lives. We navigated by them as bats use sound. Intuitive knowing arrives via energy—some elusive force that guides, leads, and directs us—and being aware of this powerful frequency was the way we were taught to conduct our lives.

In my family, the inner voice wasn't the sixth sense. It was the *first* sense, the primary guide to focus on, listen to, and follow. Situations and options were tried on like shoes, and our mother asked us, as we eventually asked ourselves, "How does this feel, energetically? Does it feel right? Does it fit? Does it seem safe, secure, and comfortable? Will it support you and provide what you really need? Does this give you good vibes?"

If we could feel and say yes, we were assured that it was the correct way to go. If we ever felt an internal no, that the vibes were uncomfortable, then we had the freedom to say so. Best of all, my mom would respect and even defend our feelings—no matter what the consequences. Each one of us grew up with a very strong, clear, and confident connection to our spiritual birthright—our intuitive knowing.

How This Applies to You

Over the years, people have asked me whether my intuition is a gift, and I've come to answer yes. But my blessing wasn't being endowed with an "extra sense." It was having a mother who created a spiritual awareness and a home environment for me that encouraged *all* of my senses to develop. For my siblings and me, and even for many other intuitive people I've known, our inner wisdom was cultivated by the permission to be more than ordinary—by a sense that as spiritual beings and children of the Universe, we could experience and receive extraordinary guidance and support in every way. I'm deeply in touch with my vibes because I was encouraged at all times to be awake, aware, and directed by my Higher Self. I grew up in a setting where intuition was treated as *normal*. It's a gift that we all inherit, that we all can experience and pass along to our own children. It's one that my husband, Patrick, and I are already handing down to our two daughters.

But what if as a child, or even as an adult, you were never given the treasure of understanding your spiritual nature or a family environment that supported this truth? Will that prevent you from being able to tap into and pass along this innate wisdom to your kids today?

Not at all. That's why I've written this book. As an intuitive teacher and guide for more than 35 years, one of the most exciting discoveries I've made is that the voice of the Inner Teacher within you can be developed at any time, once you learn how to do it. It's waiting for your recognition and attention. When it receives these, it will guide and direct you as it has led me. By first nurturing your own intuition, you'll then be able to do the same for your children.

In my many years of teaching six-sensory awareness to adults, and in my role as a mother of two intuitive daughters, I've come to believe that we can all activate a consciousness of the soul and create a spiritual home atmosphere that will foster and strengthen our most advanced perceptions. Through my own experience, I've gained a working understanding of how to cultivate profound inner guidance; and it's my greatest desire to share this knowledge with you and all families so that everyone, everywhere, can connect to the peace and creative direction we all have within us.

Awareness, Accepting, and Asking

The two most important things I've learned regarding intuition are that it's best awakened at home in the family and that it develops in three key stages. The first stage is becoming aware of your own sixth sense. Until you discover your personal inner voice, you'll leave it lying dormant, ignored, and out of reach in your and your children's lives. You must first realize that you have an internal compass in order to strengthen and benefit from it. Only then can you pass this awareness on to your sons and daughters. When a person is shown how to access intuition and is given support to *embrace* this form of guidance as valuable and valid, then it will naturally awaken and thrive and can be handed down. Therefore, the first step in helping your children connect to the wisdom of the Higher Self is to sharpen and expand your own six-sensory awareness. I'll discuss this in the first part of the book.

Accepting the gift of your intuition when it does show up in your life is the second stage of development. Simply being aware of your intuition isn't enough to help you fully embrace its profound and far-reaching benefits. You must then decide to welcome and trust the guidance you receive from your Inner Teacher, making its wisdom a deeply honored guest in your home and in your life. This means creating a state of appreciation and respect for the intuitive direction in your heart, and having the desire to enthusiastically encourage it in your family. Therefore, the second part of this book offers you practical daily routines that will help you identify and overcome obstacles to your sixth sense and aid you in recognizing and honoring intuitive feelings in all your family members.

Asking the Universe for support is the third stage in cultivating intuition at home. Requesting Divine assistance means moving beyond just being receptive to the Inner Teacher to actually seeking it as the primary guiding voice in your and your children's lives. The third part of this book teaches you and your kids how to call upon this wisdom for reliable support. It provides practices and tools that both you and your family can comfortably use to jump-start your intuition.

Opening to your inner knowing connects you to both your own spirit and to the Divine Spirit of the Universe. It takes away your sense of isolation and inadequacy, and it replaces fear with spiritual direction and confidence. When you're led by your sixth sense and an open heart, the world becomes friendly, nonadversarial, and welcoming. Life grows joyful, amusing, generous, and abundant. This is the Divine plan. The six-sensory intuitive life is one of assurance, inner peace, and creative expression. What better gift to offer yourself and your children?

PART I

Expanding Your Awareness

Your personal sixth sense is activated by training your awareness to become sharper and receive more information from others, the astral planes, your Higher Self, and God. You begin this process by learning how to expand your consciousness and better understand the way your body takes in and responds to energy. Intuitive living is the art of developing your awareness to be a highly sophisticated receiver of vibrations that will give you more accurate data to work with as you interact with people. It involves teaching yourself to be open and receptive to the subtle planes of energy that constitute our psychic lives.

The six-sensory person communes with Spirit, *sees into* rather than *looks at* things, and welcomes and responds to the guidance of God at all times. Being intuitive means becoming fully aware of your higher nature and understanding that as a spiritual being, it's your birthright to expect extraordinary levels of insight at any given time—from subtle impulses to full-blown psychic experiences such as clairaudience, clairvoyance, telepathy, and even precognition.

Awakening your sixth sense begins with an awareness of ten basic principles. They are as follows:

1. Intuition and other creative six-sensory abilities are gifts of the Divine Source within everyone.

2. We're all spiritual beings; therefore, we're all six-sensory by nature and can even be psychic.

3. Developing our innate wisdom is our spiritual birthright.

4. Intuitive insights are messages from a Divine source that lead us to our own sacred essence and our highest creative abilities.

5. Spirit-based direction benefits all people.

6. Inner guidance is activated by love and results in greater understanding and compassion for ourselves and others.

7. A six-sensory life is gentle, powerful, courageous, and always noncoercive.

8. The Inner Teacher doesn't flatter the ego; rather, it supports our spirit's expression and growth.

9. An intuitive life releases our full potential!

10. Being attuned to our sixth sense ourselves is the best way to nurture this important ability in our children.

Now that you have a clear understanding of what six-sensory intuition is, in Part I we'll focus on how you can begin to heighten your inner awareness in four basic ways:

1. First, we'll look at your family background and history and see how it may be affecting the role intuition plays in the relationship dynamics in your home today.

2. Next, we'll discuss the importance of being present for your child (or children).

3. Then we'll focus on the essential fact that intuition is a heightened awareness that originates in your heart, then moves up into your consciousness. We'll also work to strengthen this energy.

4. Finally, we'll consider your home environment; and I'll introduce ways to create a safe, inspiring atmosphere that will allow everyone living there to have a comfortably intuitive and empowered life.

Now that we know our direction, let's begin!

Chapter One

AWARENESS BEGINS WITH YOU

The Seeds Are There

The seeds of intuitive awareness lie waiting to germinate in all of us; in fact, the voice of our Higher Self is an integral, if not the most important, part of our spiritual anatomy. You can be certain that all children will demonstrate signs of their awakening intuition sooner or later. Therefore, activating this awareness in your kids isn't the challenge. The real task is providing an environment that will encourage their fledgling sixth sense to thrive. If they see you paying attention to your vibes, they'll notice and respect their own. If they hear you sharing your feelings, they'll begin to be open about their experiences as well. On the other hand, if they observe you ignoring your intuition, they'll discount theirs. In short, when you're comfortable with your sixth sense and embrace it freely and naturally as part of your spiritual makeup, then your children will, too, and they'll come to depend on it as they would any other sense.

I've observed a wide variety of family attitudes toward intuitive awareness, from the most dismissive ("It's only a coincidence!") and the highly irrational ("It's weird"), to the greatly suspicious ("You can't trust it") and flat-out rejecting ("That's ridiculous!")—and everything in between. But only in those families who believe that "the sixth sense is a natural and important part of who we are; it's the guiding voice of our Higher Self" can

5

it develop into the tool for spiritual life direction that it's intended to be.

Take a moment and reflect on your family's beliefs about inner guidance. You may recognize one of the attitudes I describe in the following sections as similar to what you experienced, and hopefully you'll become clear about how your own upbringing has influenced your intuitive potential. The point is to identify and examine the roots of your own views. This reflection will give you a sense of what you may want to build on, or perhaps overcome, to support the development of your intuition today.

The Intuitive Family

In our household, guided by my intuitive mother, decisions were driven not by logic but by what we called "vibes." Traditional reasoning wasn't abandoned altogether—it just took a backseat. My mom's intuition surfaced spontaneously and often. And when it did, she listened to it, and so did we.

I grew up in Denver, and it was our family tradition to picnic in the mountains on Sundays. I remember that on one outing, after gathering up the basket and getting ready to head home, my mother suddenly turned to my father and said, "Let's take the scenic route instead of the main highway."

My dad, who was tired, complained, "Why? It will take us an hour longer." With seven kids stuffed into the back of the car—all squabbling—he could hardly be blamed for balking.

"Because my vibes say so," my mom insisted. "Humor me, please."

Sensing that she wasn't going to give in to reason, and not wanting a fight, my father agreed to take the longer way home even though it made no sense to him.

Later that evening, my parents were watching the evening news and saw a report about an accident. A semitruck carrying hazardous material had gone out of control and overturned on the main highway at just about the time we were getting ready to leave the mountains. The road had been shut down for hours, traffic going in both directions had completely stopped, and people were stranded while the authorities attempted to clear away the dangerous mess. Meanwhile, we'd avoided the whole fiasco by taking an alternate route and were safe at home.

This kind of scenario was repeated so frequently in my family that following one's vibes seemed to me like the only natural way to do things. I've talked with a few other highly intuitive and psychic friends and clients and asked them about the prevailing attitude toward the sixth sense in their homes as they were growing up.

Kim, a student in one of my six-sensory workshops, said that her family was very intuitively centered and that they definitely expressed their inner wisdom and even described it as a physical sensation of energy.

"My mom always got a 'funny feeling' in her belly, as she called it, when the thought of someone popped into her mind—and sure enough, that person would usually phone within hours," Kim recalled. "It happened so often that we used to laugh about it and tease her to 'answer her belly-phone' because somebody was trying to reach her.

"Then there was our grandfather, her dad, who lived with us. Whenever we were faced with a decision, Papa counseled us to 'give it the tummy test' before we did anything."

My friend Elisa, who's now a holistic healer, recounted, "In our house, intuition ruled! My mother, an artist, used to say that she'd have to 'paint for inspiration' before she could find the right answer, and then she'd retreat into her studio to wait for guidance while working on a canvas. And my French grandmother, who was a fabulous cook and a real nature lover, used to tell us very clearly and with great intention that if we ever needed direction, we should just close our eyes, breathe in deeply, and 'sniff out' the right answer. 'I can always smell trouble,' she'd declare with dead seriousness as she inhaled the air, 'and so can you!'"

My dearest friend and spiritual mentor, Lu Ann Glatzmaier, is an intuitive teacher in Denver who grew up in a large Polish-Italian family of eight kids in Minnesota. Like me, she had an extremely passionate and intuitive mother, and a deeply grounded and pragmatic father. Her mom's inner direction and strong convictions set the stage for the development of Lu Ann's own gifts.

"My mother was Italian, and she was one of those babies born with a caul, a covering or veil over her face—which is a sign of a prophet in Italian culture, and she very much was one," Lu Ann told me. "Our lives were centered around her great intuition and keen observations. Her favorite expression was: 'I'll tell you how this is going to turn out,' and she'd predict the outcome of one situation after another.

"My father was a businessman, and she was able to accurately foresee the result of every deal he came up with. In spite of his frustration with my mom when she didn't tell him what he wanted to hear, he still asked for her input before he made any decision, because she was always right."

My friend Rick also grew up in a household where he was made deeply aware of his inner direction at a very young age—only *his* spiritual wisdom was sparked by his grounded *and* intuitive father.

"I remember Dad referring to his 'inner compass' as easily as he talked about the weather, and suggesting to me that I had spirit guides who looked after me and protected me as well. From watching him, I learned to look inward and ask for help, taking great comfort in knowing that it was available when I needed it," Rick recalled. "He was always checking in with his sixth sense on various matters, sometimes asking right out loud for guidance. If he got lost while driving, for instance, he'd say things like, 'Okay, spirits, get us out of this mess!' I figured if *he* could ask for direction, when generally men would never do such a thing, then so could I. And I always have."

The Nonintuitive Family

Nancy, one of my clients, experienced a much different family atmosphere. "As a child, I'd get these incredible insights about people and would occasionally share them with my mother," she said. "But my 'vibes' usually concerned my relatives or neighbors and often weren't what she wanted to hear. For example, one time

I had the distinct feeling that my Uncle Brian was broke, even though he was considered our 'rich uncle.' I told my mom, but instead of listening to me, she admonished me to 'stop making up naughty stories about people' and to 'be nice.'

"I *knew* in my heart that my instincts were correct, but I got the screwed-up message that, right or not, such feelings were impolite. So in our house intuition was frowned upon . . . it was something that upset pleasant perceptions and made my mother uneasy. It was interesting to note, however, that my uncle did end up declaring bankruptcy a year later, much to the surprise of everyone—except me.

Irene, a woman in her early 60s and a student in one of my workshops, remarked, "Growing up in my home, intuition simply didn't exist. We had an intellectual household, and our focus was solely on academics and the physical world, never on the inner, sensual side of life. I can't remember our family *ever* having a conversation that centered on anyone's emotions, let alone their intuition! Consequently, I went through life feeling as though I were blindfolded. I always sensed that something was missing, but I didn't even know what it was or where to begin looking for it."

The Anti-Intuitive Family

Gail recalls growing up in a home that was openly hostile to inner awareness. When she was about seven or eight years old, she remembers being quite intuitive—even psychic at times—but when she shared her feelings with her very conservative and religious parents, she was sent to her room to "pray and drive the demons out." Of course, this left her feeling profoundly shamed and confused.

"I just couldn't get rid of those 'demons,' as my mom called them. I saw energy fields around people, and I was telepathic. I could sometimes even sense events before they happened. I tried to warn everyone when I felt danger, but no one wanted to hear it," Gail told me.

"One time we were about to leave for my aunt's house, and suddenly I had a feeling that we should stay home. It was as though something were trying to keep me from going. I pretended that I was sick so that they'd forget about the trip, but no luck. They yelled at me to stop wasting time and get in the car. I blurted out, 'I have a bad feeling. We shouldn't go!' Sure enough, I got a dose of my father's knuckles as he told me what he thought of my 'feelings.'

"We got on the road, and about half an hour later, the sky blackened and the most frightening wind came barreling out of nowhere, pushing and pulling our car every which way. To our horror, we saw a tornado touching down. We all got out of the vehicle and ran like mad toward some trees, utterly terrified. We stayed there until the storm passed. Debris was strewn everywhere, but fortunately we were only emotionally shaken. I knew that my feelings had been a warning, but my mom and dad didn't understand. I learned to hide my vibes and tried very hard to shut them down, which I eventually succeeded in doing."

The Divided Family

No matter what your family's attitude toward intuitive and psychic feelings was, unfortunately the odds are that if you marry, you'll find yourself rooted in a new and confusing dynamic: the divided family. In this scenario, one spouse tends to be open-minded and very in touch with his or her inner guidance (six-sensory), while the other leans toward a more rational and closed point of view (five-sensory). Although, ideally, you'd use both your logic and intuition, in reality, you probably tend to prefer one of the modalities over the other and be more developed in that area. Picking a mate with an opposing preference is a natural, although usually unconscious, way of reaching for balance.

The problem arises when this dynamic becomes polarized and each partner becomes fixated on his or her own perspective to the exclusion of any other. If such a couple has children, the parent who's extremely intuitive and conceptual, but ungrounded and disorganized, will likely force the other parent to overcompensate by shutting out higher awareness altogether and becoming overly conservative and narrow-minded. The end result, not surprisingly, is two people at war with one another. I call this "One's the Gas, the Other's the Brakes" syndrome, and I've been caught in it myself from time to time.

When each spouse invalidates the other's perspective, psychic tension settles in. If such a dynamic exists in *your* house, it will cause problems that can push intuition out the door and make everyone unhappy.

This was the case for Eleanor, a highly six-sensory woman and a deeply devoted mother of three, whom she was raising full-time. She was married to a successful five-sensory structural engineer who spent a fair amount of time away from home on building projects. Eleanor worked hard to develop her intuition and psychic awareness and asked me how she could instill this kind of inner guidance in her children.

"I have to do it in such a way that my husband, Marvin, won't find out," she explained. "He thinks I'm nuts and gets annoyed when I talk to my kids about gut feelings or vibes or anything like that. He tells me that I'm 'ridiculous' and that I should 'get real.' He's so unwilling to acknowledge anything other than the physical world that I can't believe it. We argue constantly, which is exhausting. I just don't want him to hassle my kids the way he bothers me."

Eleanor had a real dilemma. She was eager for her children to develop their sixth sense and psychic perception, but at the same time wanted them to hide it from their father—quite a mixed message. Needless to say, it didn't work. Instead, the older kids shared their dad's five-sensory perspective, laughing at Eleanor's intuitive impulses while ignoring their own. But the youngest child, in loyalty to her mom, tuned in to her inner guidance, openly expressing her feelings and vibes—to the aggravation of her father and siblings. Each camp thought it was right and completely discounted the opposing point of view, setting off continual arguments and snide remarks. It was certainly unpleasant and nonproductive.

I told Eleanor that my spiritual teachers had trained me to understand that intuition *complements* reason rather than competing with or negating it, so not to argue with her husband. I suggested that she should therefore stop disregarding his opinion and listen to him instead. After all, he'd achieved a great deal in his profession that deserved respect. He couldn't be so totally unaware, as she believed, and still succeed as he'd done. He simply had a different perspective from hers—one that reflected both his strengths and blind spots.

"Strive toward a truce, Eleanor," I advised. "Imagine your family as a tree. See yourself and your youngest daughter as the leaves and branches—expansive, intuitive, and reaching out toward the unknown—while envisioning your husband and your older kids as the roots and trunk, which are grounded, protective, and anchored in the familiar. In spite of your discomfort, you complement each other. When you negate each other's perspective, you block your own ability to see the larger picture. Such intolerance for another point of view will actually work against your own sixth sense in the long run. You need to respect each other's perspective in order to create stability and encourage creative and intuitive growth in everyone.

"Open your mind and be willing to look from a broader angle," I continued. "One of the fundamentals of intuition is listening and learning all that you can about a situation, especially things you may have overlooked or don't understand or agree with, before drawing your conclusions."

Exasperated by the conflict in her home, Eleanor agreed to try this. She began by acknowledging and respecting Marvin's opinions, even though at times it was hard not to disagree or interrupt. She honestly opened her mind, and to her surprise, he even made sense on occasion.

At first, Marvin was shocked by his wife's new attitude. Then he began acting like a know-it-all, as if to say to her, "I'm glad you've come back to earth." But after a month or so, he actually approached Eleanor and asked her to check her vibes on something. She couldn't believe it! She wanted to laugh out loud at his reversal, but she restrained herself. After all those years of invalidating her sixth sense, he was now seeking it. Having been heard himself, he was now willing to listen to her. And to my client's great surprise, after she shared her inner guidance, he followed some of her suggestions.

Eleanor successfully shifted from being in a polarized standoff with her husband to enjoying mutual respect and cooperation. Eventually, their kids began to subtly reflect the change in their parents' attitudes as well. The youngest moved toward more objectivity, asking her father questions more often rather than quickly dismissing him as her mother used to do. And the two older children started asking Eleanor for her vibes in the name of "good fun" more frequently than before.

Heated deadlocks in a family are very frustrating because they lead people to invalidate each other and set up unnecessary competition and tension. Fortunately, awakening your sixth sense doesn't require you to reject or ignore reason, nor does it ask you to tune out your other five senses. Intuition isn't irrational, although it can appear to be so at times, especially if you only consider the obvious and physical side of things and aren't in the habit of looking or listening for the more subtle or hidden aspects of life.

Although this may come as a surprise, most intuitive people are also the most practical and reasonable souls you'll ever encounter. This is because the sixth sense works best when we're well informed by our other senses. One of my favorite definitions of *intuition* is "paying attention." This is a good one, because paying attention is the key to heightened awareness. God didn't set up our spiritual abilities to compete with our physical ones. And similarly, the five senses aren't intended to negate the sixth one, but to complement and support it.

Understanding and creating harmonious family dynamics is essential if you want to nurture intuition at home, because as long as polarized standoffs exist, spiritual awareness won't be able to flourish either in yourself or your household. While this sort of opposition is present—whether between spouses or between parents and children—you and your family will undoubtedly be too caught up in struggle to notice and trust inner guidance enough to benefit from it.

Reality Check: Intuition Awareness Quiz

On a separate sheet of paper, take the following quiz to see where you are in relationship to your sixth sense today and to look at whether or not you or your family members are interfering with each other's intuitive growth. For each question, answer *Rarely, Sometimes,* or *Never.*

old   *new*

2 1. I'm aware of how my children and I feel around certain people. *3*

3 (2.) I trust my first impressions about individuals and situations. *3*

3 3. I easily notice my intuitive feelings. *3*

2 4. I speak openly and comfortably about inner guidance at home. *3*

5. I follow my instincts no matter what my family members think. *3*

6. The attitudes of my loved ones greatly affect how much I trust my intuition. *2*

7. I can change my mind and decisions easily if I get a gut feeling to do so, even if it will upset someone close to me. *3*

8. I can sense when people are in trouble, especially my kids and other relatives. *3*

9. There are lots of coincidences in my life, particularly concerning my family. *3*

10. My partner and children respect my intuition, and I honor and listen to theirs. *3*

11. I go with my hunches even if I receive conflicting advice. 3

12. I can stand up to opposing energy, for either myself or my kids. 3

13. I look to my inner guidance first and last when making decisions, and encourage my children to do the same. 3

14. I make no attempt to hide my intuitive feelings, especially in my home or with my spouse, partner, or parents. 3

When you've completed the quiz, go back and look at your answers. Give yourself:

- 1 point for each *Never*
- 2 points for each *Rarely*
- 3 points for each *Sometimes*

If your score was 1–15:
Apparently you weren't taught to listen to or value your sixth sense as a child, so it's no surprise that you hesitate to do so today. Perhaps you've attracted a partner who *does* value intuition, although this may make you nervous or feel threatening at times. Don't worry—your internal compass is simply lying dormant, waiting to be activated and put to good use. You'll begin to relax and embrace it as you practice using the tools in the following chapters.

If your score was 16–30:
You were probably made aware of intuition when you were young, but most likely lived in an environment that was ambivalent or opposed it. Perhaps you're now experiencing a polarized dynamic with your partner or family members, flip-flopping daily between confidence and doubt. Be encouraged by the fact that

simply being aware of your vibes goes a long way toward strengthening them. As you avoid conflicts with your spouse and use good humor and a respectful approach, your entire family will soon delight in the wonderful benefits of inner awareness.

If your score was 31–42:

You are undoubtedly one of those people who was gifted with relatives who nurtured your sixth sense, and you're probably well on your way to passing this blessing on to your children. Celebrate this treasure as you expand even more in sharing your inner wisdom and vision with your family.

Ending a Polarized Viewpoint and Establishing Harmony

No matter what your beliefs were growing up, and even if you find yourself in a polarized situation in your family today, you can still develop your own intuition and foster it in your children as well. With awareness and by using a gentle approach, you can begin to help all your loved ones experience the healing benefits of inner guidance without creating conflict.

As I mentioned, the best way to cultivate intuition at home is to stop arguing over opinions, and instead work toward understanding and enjoying the sixth sense. If antagonistic or negative attitudes about this subject are a problem in your household, there are several ways to eliminate them and move back into balance. The first step is to ask yourself if *you* are the one with a polarizing or dismissive perspective.

Checking In . . .

- Are you overly analytical and focused on the physical world?

- Do you have a strongly critical view of intuition?

- Do you deny the unseen, hidden aspects of life?

If so, you may be a rationalist or have adopted some of the negative beliefs about the sixth sense that your family of origin held. If you believe that this is the case, practice noticing new things and begin looking beyond appearances for the nuances and more subtle aspects of the lives of your spouse and kids. You can:

- Try to observe something new about each member of your family.

- Invite them to do the same.

- Recognize that your intuition is like a muscle that needs workouts to remain sharp, accurate, and open.

- Ask yourself whether you're controlling and if you avoid certain situations and people because you may not be able to take charge of them.

Discovering New Territory

Inviting intuition into your home is definitely asking for something new and powerful to come into your life, and it requires that you open up and relax your grip a bit. Practice doing this in little ways every day.

- Try taking a different route to work.

- Go on a spontaneous outing.

- Practice listening to other family members respectfully.

- Play *I Spy*, the kids' game in which the players seek to notice the things hidden in the world around them.

Get the Facts First

Consciously ease up and practice separating your fears from the facts. Many people mistake their worries for reality, and in the name of "logic," they irrationally draw all kinds of narrow-minded and inaccurate conclusions. Actively train yourself to notice what *is* real, and don't let a defensive or reactive mind-set distort situations or confuse your judgment. If you have young children, up to about four or five years of age, observe their way of looking at life, because they're very good at seeing what *is* without editing or making misguided interpretations of things. They just accept life. They experience the moment and don't get caught up in projections, transference, and defenses. They're simply aware of the here and now, paying very close attention to all that's going on around them. Follow their example, for they have something to teach you.

Don't Be an Intuitive Snob

If, on the other hand, you're somewhat intuitive now and feel disrespected, misunderstood, or invalidated by your partner or some other family member, then ask yourself if you're unconsciously treating them in the same way.

Ask Yourself . . .

- Do I act like a spiritual know-it-all, discounting others who seem disconnected from their inner guidance?

- Do I secretly think I'm a more evolved, enlightened being among mere mortals?

- Do I fail to appreciate the grounding and stability that my more practical intimates give me?

- Do I use my intuition as a way to tune people out or invalidate their opinions?

- Do I ignore individuals who reject or disagree with me and consider them bad, stupid, or wrong?

- Do I get angry and resentful toward those who don't accept my higher awareness as natural, and "punish" them with my negative judgments?

I've noticed that some budding six-sensories quickly adopt an attitude of superiority toward those who remain disconnected from their own intuition (five-sensories), who ironically *do* pick up on the disdain and resent it. Ask yourself if you're being recklessly ungrounded and disrespectful of others, especially when they think you're acting crazy about your vibes.

For example, my husband and I used to have a running battle about my refusal to lock our doors. I intuitively felt that we were safe and said so, but he finally made a very good point that got through to me. "Trust the Universe, Sonia," Patrick told me, "but don't tempt it!"

He was right, and I now lock the doors.

Be Considerate

Intuition shows up spontaneously, often requiring quick, decisive responses and even abrupt changes in plans if you follow its guidance. This sort of unpredictability can upset some people and arouse their fears. You may collide head-on with the anxieties of other family members if you aren't careful and considerate about sharing your gut feelings, especially if you ask them to follow your lead. I've found that simply by being sensitive and introducing your insights to others gently, and even with humor, you often clear the way for intuition to enter your family dynamic. When my inner voice suggests sudden change, I explain to my husband and daughters that my vibes are sending signals that might "rock the boat," and ask for their help and cooperation. My earnest request is usually all they need to agree to accept my vibes and follow them, even when they don't want to.

A case in point occurred just recently when we were waiting in the Chicago airport to fly to London to spend Thanksgiving weekend together. The flight was delayed, and we waited several hours. Then suddenly, just before we were finally asked to board, my vibes told me, "Stay home." Not expecting the abrupt change of plans, I looked at everybody and said, "I can't explain why, but I just got bad vibes. Would you guys mind if we didn't go?"

Shocked, but used to such scenarios, they seemed at once frustrated, confused, disappointed, and even scared. However, in spite of all their jumbled emotions, they looked at each other and agreed, saying, "Okay, let's go home," without asking any questions. I did have to sit in their silence on the drive back, which wasn't fun, especially since at that moment I had no way of justifying my request, but they still didn't give me any resistance.

The next morning, we found out that the plane we were supposed to take had landed just fine, which didn't support my decision. But to our surprise, an hour later my sister in Chicago had an emergency in her house and needed us to help her out. We all agreed that given the choice between spending three days in London or being there for my sister at a time of extreme distress, we were glad we'd stayed home.

Requesting support for your intuition rather than imposing it on your family fosters goodwill, and often shifts a negative person into a more positive and receptive frame of mind. At least it did in my family. Whenever my mother had a vibe, she asked us to "humor her" by listening, especially when it meant inconveniencing us. It worked for her, it works for me, and I'm betting it will do the trick for you, too.

Laughter and Play

Another way to overcome a polarized or critical attitude toward intuition in your family is to approach it in a lighthearted, playful way that encourages everyone to join in and discuss their own vibes. Avoid making the subject too heavy or serious and you'll get far better results when it comes to gaining respect and cooperation.

My client Robert was very six-sensory and felt that his sons were, too, but he was frustrated because his wife, Ruth, completely negated his gut feelings and discouraged him when he asked their kids to voice theirs, laughing at all of them as "ridiculous." He often invited his children to share their dreams at the breakfast table and attempt to interpret them together, to which Ruth's response was, "Stop wasting your time on all that! You have to get to work, they need to go to school, and there's no room for this nonsense or you'll all be late."

"She shuts me down and takes all the fun out of our psychic explorations," Robert complained.

The problem was that my client and his sons never really invited her to join in the fun. The parents' relationships with their boys had become polarized, with Ruth focused on making sure everyone's work got done, and Robert concentrating on play and the inner life.

"Do you ever ask Ruth about her vibes, feelings on things, or dreams?" I asked him.

"No way," he answered emphatically. "She wouldn't know a vibe from a hole in the head, and I'm convinced she doesn't dream."

"That's the problem right there. You're shutting her down."

"Me? How? *She's* the one with the closed mind."

"True," I said, "but you're so convinced that what *you* know about her is all there is to know that you're actually preventing her from exploring any other side of herself freely. You and the kids are boxing her in, and she's angry that she's being left out. That's why she doesn't play along. My teacher Dr. Tully once said that one of the best ways to sharpen your own intuition is to never assume you know someone or something completely. Always leave room for surprise—in your case, even with your wife."

"Let me think about that," Robert said. Then after a moment, he asked, "So what should I do?"

"Invite her to join in. Ask her about her vibes and tell her it's only a game. Don't be heavy, and act interested in what she has to say."

"Okay," he agreed, "but I doubt it will make any difference."

21

The next time I saw Robert, he painted quite a different picture of his wife and the family atmosphere. "I took your advice, even though I had my doubts, and encouraged the boys to start asking Ruth what her vibes were on everything. At first she resisted, but we didn't give up—teasing, prodding, and having great fun with her—and she finally started to open up. To our astonishment, she shared some wonderful, incredible, and even psychic feelings with us. We were all so amazed that she had it in her. It turned our ideas about who she is upside down. Even she admitted that she was surprised to find she had so much unacknowledged insight. Intrigued, she began paying more attention to her intuition, although she's always conservative in how she voices it, and now our whole family dynamic has completely changed."

The Stick-in-the-Mud

Even if you apply my suggestions, there will always be some people who are so stuck in their point of view that they stubbornly refuse to shift into higher awareness, playful or otherwise. They may be closed-minded spouses, old-fashioned parents, or even cynical children. No matter how good your intentions to help them activate their inner guidance and join you in the fun and gifts this brings, the chances are that you may still find someone who will resist.

For instance, my client Polly, who was married to an accountant, was a massage therapist and the mother of two teenagers, ages 17 and 19. Through her studies and her bodywork practice, Polly really awakened her intuition and began excitedly sharing this awareness with her kids, who in turn started to sense and express their own vibes more freely. They were having a great adventure and were benefiting from it enormously.

But although they encouraged dad to join in, he was completely turned off by the whole world of six-sensory insight and absolutely refused to join in. He was openly disgusted with all of them and said so. Polly's husband was stuck on the old messages he received from his superstitious mother and his overly analytical father, who taught him that intuitive information isn't spiritual or valid. A fundamentalist Christian and a conservative businessman, Polly's husband found the idea of vibes too threatening to accept. Until he could gain an understanding to the contrary, he'd maintain his suspicion and negative judgments.

I suggested to Polly that given the situation, this was her opportunity to move into the role of spiritual teacher with him, just as she was doing for her children, and that the best way to accomplish this would be to assume a neutral, nonjudgmental, patient attitude toward his beliefs, but not let his harsh perceptions distract her from her positive experiences. I advised her to treat him with quiet acceptance, recognizing that he was afraid and that his fear wasn't something she needed to wrestle with. I encouraged her to instead stay the course, continue to openly share her feelings with her kids, and perhaps even keep on discussing the positive benefits the three of them were experiencing—but in a low-key, noncoercive way, while politely ignoring her husband's potshots. "Eventually, he'll tire of throwing them at you if he doesn't get a reaction," I told her. "Just smile and say 'I love you' whenever he attacks, and patiently go about your business."

I had just a few more suggestions for Polly: "When sharing your vibes, try using language that's less likely to threaten him. It could very well be that the words you choose, like *spirit, vibes,* and so forth, might trigger some sort of negative reaction in him that he just can't help. Try using more commonplace phrases, such as 'I'll bet,' 'It's a gut feeling,' 'I have a hunch,' or 'It seems to me,' when expressing your intuition. You may get less emotionally charged resistance from him.

"And most important, remain loving toward him. After all, the most important role the sixth sense plays in your life is to teach you to see and appreciate the true nature of people and things, even when others can't. The fact is that he's a spiritual being who's capable of receiving personal inner guidance just like the rest of us, even if he doesn't know or feel it right now. His reaction to your vibes is a reflection of where he is spiritually at this point—not a real judgment of you or your kids. So don't set yourself up for trouble by demanding that he recognize something that he's not quite able to accept yet. After all, if he were blind, you wouldn't get angry that he couldn't see; and if he were deaf, you wouldn't be annoyed that he couldn't hear. The sixth sense is just as important as the other natural senses, and obviously his is somewhat disabled for now, so be compassionate. Accept his attitude as a handicap, and be patient with him."

In Polly's case, the suggestions worked. She stopped trying to convince her husband to open up. She changed her vocabulary and simply ignored his rude and negative comments. She called me one day to report that just as I'd predicted, he had, in fact, mellowed out, and eventually his criticism had faded away. "It's as though we have an unspoken agreement to tolerate one another on the matter," she said. "Now when the kids and I tell each other about our vibes and other intuitive experiences, he doesn't leave the room like he used to. Instead, he picks up the paper and pretends to read, or turns on the TV, but we all suspect that he's really listening and is interested, and it makes us smile."

When you're around someone who's as stuck as Polly's husband was, avoid trying to change or reform their attitude—or worse yet, ganging up on them. That will only make them even more resistant, and it will make you look and feel controlling. The sixth sense awakens from the *inside,* and is never sparked by an argument or attack from someone else. Let your own positive and peaceful way of life—with its synchronicities, "Aha!" moments, and delightful gifts—speak for itself. A family is a very tight unit, and even the most narrow-minded member will take note of changes and improvements in you. If you resist invaliding another's point of view, no matter how tempting it may be, he or she is far more likely to eventually accept yours.

Establishing New Habits

- Approach intuition with a loving, playful attitude. Keep your ego out of it.

- Ask your parents or other relatives if you have any intuitive or psychic ancestors.

- Be respectful and even-tempered toward all family members' opinions about inner guidance—even those with closed minds.

- Avoid drama when sharing your vibes with your loved ones. Intuition is natural, so don't be theatrical or weird.

- Be tolerant and good-humored if a family member behaves in a skeptical way toward your or anyone else's spiritual compass.

- Steer clear of all "campaigns of reform."

- Encourage your partner and children to check in with their gut feelings when making decisions.

- Know that intuition is latent in all of us, even if others seem dismissive or unaware of it.

- Resist being a know-it-all or having a superior attitude when it comes to your sixth sense!

- Listen to and honor everyone's vibes, even the subtle ones of the youngest children.

- No matter what your personal history is, know that you can cultivate the seeds of intuition in all your family members today, through awareness, acceptance, and action.

Reflections

Take a moment and reflect on your own family background and the beliefs about six-sensory perception that you grew up with. Ponder the following questions to better understand your personal intuitive foundation.

- What was your mother's attitude toward inner guidance?

- Did she freely express her feelings, or did she hide them?

- If she was open about her vibes, what value did she place on them? (For example, did she listen to them, or did she invalidate or dismiss them?)

- Was she superstitious about the messages from her sixth sense?

- Did she follow her internal wisdom, or did she defer to the feelings of your father or some other person?

- Was she confident or insecure?

- Can you talk about intuition with your mom today?

- Do you share her beliefs about this topic, or do you have different views?

- What was your father's attitude toward intuition?

- Was he in touch with his inner guidance? Did he ever express his vibes?

- Did he allow you to be six-sensory?

- How did he respond to your mother's or to your intuitive feelings if you discussed them? Did he take them seriously or did he invalidate them?

- Can you talk about spiritual awareness with your dad?

- Do you share his beliefs about intuition, or do you have a different perspective?

- How do you feel about intuition today?

- What insights from your answers to all these questions might help you lay a stronger foundation to support vibes in yourself and your family?

Now that you have some tools for dealing with resistance to six-sensory ways of being, we'll take a look at how becoming more present and paying closer attention to the world around you can sharpen your intuitive abilities.

Chapter Two

BEING PRESENT

So many people have the false notion that following your intuition means tuning out the real world, but nothing could be further from the truth. As strange as it may seem, in order to become aware of your sixth sense, first it's necessary to be mindful of the environment around you and fully conscious of what's here and now. My spiritual teacher Dr. Tully taught me that the key to developing inner knowing is to pay attention to what's happening in the world around you. He told me that those who think that receiving spiritual guidance is about tuning in to some otherworldly frequency are confused.

"Genuine intuition," he explained, "is founded on accurate observations of current reality. It's this information, when turned over to the higher mind, that leads to the most advanced insights." In other words, you need to be completely present in the moment to activate your vibes.

Many of us today, especially parents, are so overbooked— juggling too many things at one time, constantly playing catch-up, and racing around like crazy—that we often end up diminishing our awareness to nothing more than a whirling gray fog. When we're so overwhelmed and exhausted, we can't see the most obvious of details, let alone tune in to the more subtle, intuitive aspects of life.

One day many years ago, when my children were only one and two years old, I sat on the front porch, feeling bone tired after a long day at work, and watched the girls playing in front of the house while my husband watered the lawn. After a few minutes, a pleasant-looking woman walked up to Patrick, and the two of them chatted briefly. Then she smiled at me and continued down the street.

"Who's that, Patrick?" I asked.

He looked at me in disbelief. "Sonia, she's our neighbor and has been living next door to us for the past six months." He shook his head in wonder that I didn't recognize her.

"You're kidding," I said. "I've never seen her before."

"Yes, you have!" he insisted. "Hundreds of times. You've just never paid *attention* to her until now."

Boy, did I ever feel like a fool. Patrick was right. My awareness had truly shriveled up in the past few months. Since my second daughter, Sabrina, had been born, my life had sped up so much that it had become a blur. At that time, I spent my days trying to manage so much—taking care of two girls in diapers, renovating our two-flat building with Patrick while he worked two jobs, keeping up my one-on-one work with clients, and giving workshops. All of this was crammed into what felt like very short days, and I was so overwhelmed by my many activities that sometimes I couldn't even remember what *I* had done, let alone be conscious of anyone else. And now, staring at a neighbor as if she were a complete stranger, I realized that in my effort to do it all, I'd spiraled right out of my own body and off of planet Earth. I was so "otherly" focused that I'd lost the ability to see beyond my own nose.

Although Patrick and I laughed about it at the time, that experience was a true wake-up call for me. *Where am I? Where have I been? Where's my awareness lately?* I wondered. As I reflected on the previous year, I could hardly bring any of it into focus. Nothing stood out. As I watched my daughters scrutinizing the ants on the sidewalk, I realized that with all my hurried doings, I hadn't *really* been present in my life . . . not to them, not to anything.

I observed my girls gleefully examining a fallen leaf. First Sonia eyeballed it very closely, then handed it to Sabrina, who promptly popped it in her mouth. It felt good to be back in the present, leaving my mental rat race behind. I took in a long, deep breath, savoring the air as it filled my lungs and energized me. As I exhaled and sat in that quiet moment before my next inhalation, my awareness exploded into a symphony of intense sensuality. I began to notice things I hadn't before. Colors became brighter, and sounds more acute. My children were no longer just extensions of me, but were once again unique and precious beings. It was as if someone had tuned my mind's TV channel from fuzzy black-and-white to sharp, brilliant color.

Slowly, even luxuriously, I took another breath. Sonia tottered toward me, screaming, "Mommy, look!" Sabrina spit out her leaf and followed her sister. Then Sonia held up her baby hand to me, and right in the middle of her palm was a bright, orange-red ladybug with black dots. The minute I looked, it flew away.

In that moment, I decided that I absolutely had to *slow down!* I needed to stop racing around in my mind, frantically trying to cover all the bases. I had to quit scheduling my day down to the nanosecond, leaving myself no time to be conscious of anything. Finally, I saw how crucial it was to let go of my nose-to-the-grindstone, hyperdrive quest to keep it all together, and simply breathe and trust that my relaxed pace wouldn't compromise anything. In fact, it was necessary if I wanted to be a good mother, and more important, give my children vital life tools such as intuition and clear vision. I had to curtail the insane and unconscious rush to do it all that had obliterated my awareness of my world.

So this is what Dr. Tully meant when he said intuition arises out of a keen sense of the here and now, I thought as I watched Sabrina digging in the dirt and Sonia very carefully sticking her toes under the water sprinkler. *They're noticing everything in this moment by having a direct experience of the world around them . . . right now! This is where inner guidance is born. This is the first lesson in consciousness.*

Stay in the Moment

Noticing and experiencing your surroundings requires an acute presence of mind. Babies are born with this ability. They watch everything deeply, closely, and carefully. They don't miss a thing.

But what do *we,* the rushed, preoccupied, overextended parents, see? If your life is like mine used to be, the answer is "Not much." And if you don't pay attention to the world, how well informed can you be? The less you know about your circumstances, the less likely you are to draw the right conclusions and make the best decisions for yourself and for your children. In order to foster intuition, you must sharpen your awareness and learn about the nature of things around you—and that requires allowing enough *time* to do so.

I'm very sympathetic to moms and dads who have heavy schedules, because being a parent, especially a working one, involves so much planning. I know it's hard to stay in the moment, but there are things you can do to slow down and be present for your kids, even while you struggle to keep up with life's demands. The first step you can take is to meditate.

Meditation

Meditation is the most effective way to slow down and sharpen your awareness because it clears away the mental noise and distractions that prevent you from noticing what's important in the here and now. This practice helps you become more at ease, balanced, and present in the moment. Best of all, it stretches time and seems to give you more of it. Don't ask me how because I don't know, but I'm certain that it works. Try it and see for yourself! And if you've never meditated, don't worry. It's not difficult—it's simply the art of relaxing your body, resting your emotions, and quieting your mind for 15 minutes a day. There are no tricks to doing this, but you can use various techniques to make it easier, including the following:

Let's meditate . . .

Meditation begins with focusing on your breath.
Start by taking in a deep one right now . . . through
your nose and out your mouth . . . and let out the sound
aah. . . . Notice how much your awareness expands simply
by doing this. Take a few more full, cleansing breaths, then
allow yourself to settle into an easy, rhythmic pattern.

Next, gently close your eyes. Notice the difference
that just removing visual stimulation makes in your
level of relaxation. With your eyes shut, continue to
breathe in to the count of four, hold it for a count
of four, then exhale to the count of four.

If thoughts arise during this exercise, simply witness
them and then go back to your breath. Don't fight or
struggle with each emerging thought. See it as one
of a string of train cars moving through the night,
entering and then drifting out of your consciousness.

Continue breathing and relaxing for 15 minutes,
then gently open your eyes and go about your day.

That's it—you've just meditated! Doing so for 15 minutes a day is all it takes to clear your mind, heighten your awareness, and bring yourself fully into the moment. To deepen your experience, you may want to repeat a few calming phrases as you breathe, such as *I am* . . . on the inhale and . . . *at peace* on the exhale. Or you might like to play some ambient or classical music (such as Vivaldi or Pachelbel) softly in the background to help you quiet your mind even more. The best way to meditate successfully is to make it a daily habit. It's far more effective to set aside 15 minutes at the same time every day than to do it randomly once a week for an hour.

A busy parent's schedule does make it tricky to develop a consistent practice, so you'll have to be both creative and practical in figuring out what works best for you. I personally prefer meditating in the morning before getting out of bed—I simply prop myself up on my pillow and begin. This routine was sometimes a challenge when my kids were very young because, as we all know, they usually wake up before we do. On those days, I seized the moment while they took a nap.

You'll have to find a time that suits you as well. Just remember, it's only 15 minutes, and not only do you deserve it, you *need* it. Besides, meditation is an ongoing gift for both you and your family because with regular practice, you'll become more aware and intuitive and have far greater patience.

My client Louise, a mother of twin boys who works part-time, learned that the best time for her to meditate was just after putting her sons down for their afternoon nap. They got to rest, and so did she. Joan, another working mom with teenage girls, found that she could only steal a few minutes for herself during her lunch hour, because there was never a free moment or enough quiet at home. My friend Mark meditated in his car for 15 minutes after work. He parked in the garage, giving his family strict instructions not to bother him until he came into the house. Everyone soon adjusted to his routine and appreciated his far less cranky, more attentive frame of mind when he finally went inside. Sometimes, however, even 15 minutes is asking too much. In that case, here's your backup plan.

The Ten-Second Meditation

Try this: When you're under stress, overwhelmed, rushed, or preoccupied, with no time for a real break, simply touch the thumb and forefinger of each hand together and say quietly to yourself, *I am* . . . as you inhale, and . . . *calm* as you exhale. Allow the word *calm* to reverberate throughout your entire body. The act of connecting thumbs to forefingers is a physical reminder to come back to the moment, and the phrase *I am calm* washes away your tension. Teach your kids to do this as well. (They'll like it because it's easy.)

Simplify and Slow Down

Another way to be more present in your life is to simplify your commitments and allow yourself more time to relax. Part of the reason why some of us are so unaware and distracted is simply that we're juggling too many balls at once. In trying to keep up with all of our obligations, we never have a moment to unwind.

For example, my client Josephine ran her own dressmaking business while parenting three boys, ages 7, 9, and 13. She also ran the PTA, taught yoga classes twice a week, belonged to a book club, and helped her husband with his real-estate business as a part-time secretary—in addition to taking her kids to soccer games, basketball tournaments, and piano lessons. She never went anywhere without her cell phone, portfolio, and beeper, plus a to-do list from here to the end of the next millennium.

Initially, Josephine prided herself on her ability to manage so much, but eventually she began to show signs of stress. She finally came to see me for an appointment because she was having memory lapses, forgetting appointments, losing patience, spacing out, and generally confusing her commitments at an ever-increasing rate. In addition, she had migraines and was developing irritable bowel syndrome. Her symptoms were frightening to her and were causing difficulties for everyone who depended on her.

"Sonia, do you think I'm all right?" she asked me anxiously. "I'm so forgetful and temperamental that I'm out of control. I have no patience with the boys. I yell at them all the time and can hardly stand to be with them because they're so loud and rambunctious. I'm not myself at all."

It didn't take any great effort on my part to see how absolutely overcommitted Josephine was and to understand that this was the source of her problem. Her memory lapses and confusion were her mind's way of managing the overload. In her zealousness to "do it all," she was, in fact, accomplishing less than ever. Driven by her ambitious desire to achieve everything, she was also depriving herself of the ability to fully experience anything.

"Josephine, slow down!" I told her. "You need to cut back, prioritize, and delegate. I'm sorry to say that you'll just have to let some things go—at least if you want to become more grounded and intuitive. You're doing way too much, and your breakneck pace is destroying your capacity to be present for anything. You're not enjoying your family or life; and for all your efforts, you've only succeeded in becoming miserable and exhausted. When was the last time you had a casual conversation with one of your sons—or played a game, read a book together, or simply hung out with them?" I asked.

"I can't remember," she sighed. "I'm too busy working and feel impatient when I think about everything I have to do. I don't even want to be with them. I just yearn to be alone."

"So *do* take some time out, even for just a few minutes a day," I suggested. "That feeling is your spirit knocking on your door, telling you what you need. If you don't pay attention, soon you won't be able to focus on *anything*."

Josephine was in dire need of a change. I therefore advised her to take an objective, ruthless look at her schedule and eliminate everything that wasn't a matter of life or death. It didn't take a lot of persuasion because she was so scared of her health deteriorating further. In the process, she noticed that she'd packed her days so tightly that she'd barely left herself time to breathe.

Once Josephine admitted the problem, she decided to make a few changes. She let go of her secretarial work and her yoga classes and set up a more realistic timetable for herself. She arranged car pools, hired a teenage girl to work a few hours a week in her office, and resigned from the PTA position. She decided that every day from 3 to 4 would be her hour to relax and warned everyone not to bother her then unless it was a real emergency.

Once she created some breathing room, she (not surprisingly) lightened up. She began to like her husband again instead of resenting him, and she even became more inspired in her dress-design work, which allowed her to raise her prices and increase her cash flow. The best part, however, was the much-improved and genuine connection she began to feel with her sons. She set aside an hour a week for one-on-one time with each of them.

In Josephine's case, less was clearly more. By drastically cutting back her activities and slowing down, she got out of her head and reconnected to her spirit, heart, family, and life. "It wasn't easy to get out of the rat race," she said, "but it wasn't as hard as I thought it would be. And everyone seems to be happier for it—especially me."

Be Interested

I truly believe that one of the bedrocks of helping people— especially your children—develop their sixth sense is showing your interest and care. I've noticed that a number of immensely creative and highly intuitive people had at least one nurturing, dedicated adult to guide them. Steven Spielberg, for example, had a mother who was very supportive of his passions. She helped him make his earliest movies, even taking him out of school at times to do so. And in the case of Jane Goodall, the famous primate anthropologist, it was her mom who cleared a major obstacle that allowed her to go to Tanzania to study wild chimpanzees in 1960. At that time, it was unheard of for a young woman (Jane was 26) to go by herself to live among the animals in Africa, and the British authorities refused to let her go until her mother volunteered to accompany her for the first three months.

Many of my six-sensory intuitive friends have also had highly present and interested parents. As I've already mentioned, my friend and mentor Lu Ann, a gifted intuitive and a spiritual scholar, had a mother who readily shared Lu's passion for philosophical inquiry and a father who was more than happy to engage in deep discussions with her. Similarly, my friend Ron, a musician and composer, had a very attentive and aware father who bought him his first guitar the minute he noticed his son's love for music; and he has enthusiastically listened to every original composition Ron has written since the third grade.

Of course I'm convinced that my own upbringing provided the foundation for the strong development of my gifts. My mom was always present and listened to and enjoyed being with her children. She laughed, joked, danced, and talked with us for hours. We looked forward to telling her about our days after school because she truly wanted to know how they had gone. Even the neighborhood kids came over to our house to have conversations with her. She and I shared a special passion for all things psychic. One of our favorite pastimes was discussing vibes and Spirit, and to this day, we continue to enjoy it.

I recently heard a National Public Radio report on orphans in Romania that mentioned how a lack of interest and attention had affected their lives. The first thing researchers discovered was that, on average, when these children grew up, their IQs were 50 percent lower than those of adults who'd been raised in loving and affectionate families. The orphans—even those who'd received some remedial help later—also had smaller brains and heads than their peers unless they'd gotten support before the age of nine.

If lowered IQs and decreased brain size are the result of inadequate attention, we can hardly expect a children's higher intuitive faculties to thrive unless they receive excellent care. It's no wonder that kids are so good at getting attention, because they desperately need it. When we give them genuine, positive encouragement, delighting in their spirit and sharing their world with them, their inner awareness blossoms like a flower in the sun—and so does ours.

Be creative in finding ways to be more present for your children today. Talk *with* them, not *at* them. Ask them how they feel, especially about their vibes regarding the things happening in their world. Explain to them that their sixth sense is natural and that we all have a quiet inner voice that speaks in our heart, guiding and protecting us throughout our lives if only we listen and follow it. Don't be surprised if your kids readily understand what you mean. After all, they're born with a strong connection to this innate wisdom, and you don't have to do much to get them to talk about it. They're conscious of their intuitive feelings and will be glad to share them with you if you're interested and open about your own.

If your life is jam-packed with obligations, get out your appointment book and find time to be with your family members before you commit your entire schedule to everyone else. Take a few moments to be with your loved ones before you fall exhausted into bed, letting them know that they're worth your time and attention. Make it one of your top priorities to have the energy and presence of mind to listen to their experiences and concerns before they go to sleep.

I know that many parents today were raised with the belief that you can't play until your work is done. However, today we know that our to-do list will never be finished and that we must carve out the time to have fun. As a matter of fact, one of the most brilliant intuitive thinkers of the 20th century, Albert Einstein, considered play his most important pursuit. After he died, several scientists examined his brain to see how it differed from those of others and discovered that both the left and right hemispheres were far more highly developed than most people's and that he had grown many more glial cells, which help in the transmission of signals in the nervous system and play a role in intuitive awareness.

The researchers had been inspired to study Einstein's brain by an earlier experiment, in which scientists had placed one group of rats in a sterile environment that provided only food and water and offered no playful stimulation. A second group was put in a virtual Disneyland that included wheels, mazes, and other entertaining activities. As suspected, the deprived animals not only didn't grow any new glial cells in their brains, but they actually lost 20 percent of the ones they'd started with. Furthermore, their awareness and intuition diminished, and they became sickly and weak. In contrast, the rats that were given fun things to do experienced a 30 percent increase in their number of glial cells. They were far more resourceful, creative, and healthy than the rats that had been put in the impoverished setting. It was an amazing discovery!

The scientists who investigated Einstein's brain concluded that his intense and relentless pursuit of play had led to the development of the all-important glial cells, an essential component that contributed to his intuitive and creative genius. They also inferred that anyone who adds more enjoyable, stimulating activities to their lives will also grow more glial cells, thus significantly increasing their imaginative and six-sensory capabilities.

By engaging in daily play, Einstein changed the face of the world. Who knows what marvelous achievements will come about if you encourage your own little geniuses, and even yourself, to experience more pleasure and recreation. With this potential in mind, don't you think it's worth rethinking your lifestyle? If you put off the joys of sharing creative time with yourself and your children until you've finished your work, you risk missing out on everything, including the chance to develop more amazing glial cells. This would be an irrevocable loss for all of you.

You don't need large amounts of time to have fun with your kids and share their world. Even five minutes of quality presence and play is worth hours of preoccupied effort. For your own spiritual well-being and intuitive growth, allow yourself the leisure to actually get to know and enjoy these light beings who are your children.

The Family Dinner

One of the simplest yet most overlooked ways to be present for your family is to recapture the tradition of the evening meal. It's remarkable to me how many people today have thrown that custom to the winds. Some have completely forgotten the ritual of togetherness and spiritual bonding that can unfold at the table. They erroneously believe that meals are only about physical sustenance and that any drive-through will do. The prevailing attitude is: "Everyone for him- or herself!"

On the contrary, the family dinner should feed the soul as well as the body. Ideally, it offers an opportunity to notice, enjoy, celebrate, and encourage everyone's experiences, challenges, and contributions. It can be a time of genuine connection, when you and your kids have the pleasure of delighting in each other's company and communicating what's going on in your lives. It shouldn't be an occasion to air your differences, and is never the place to argue.

When I was growing up, the dinner table was a place where we shared stories, told jokes, and discovered what each of us was up to. It was central to our developing a sense of ourselves, and we looked forward to it. With nine of us, it required real cooperation and attention for everyone to feel heard, but we managed. It was not only an opportunity to practice presence, but to learn to listen as well.

"But I'm too busy to cook!" is the despairing cry of many over-worked parents. Take heart: The meal doesn't need to be home-cooked (although fresh food that's lovingly prepared is no doubt the best). Nor must it be put together by one person. You can order in, go out, or whip something up together. Make it a democratic event, asking everyone to participate. The point is to value and preserve the family dinner as a time for healing your bodies and spirits. Let it be a chance to share ideas, stories, and news and to be present. Create this ritual to stop the clock and be here now . . . don't throw away this precious opportunity!

Presence Lends Power

If you don't think that the presence and awareness of parents makes a difference in helping your children tap into their inner strength and resources, let me tell you a story about how my daughter Sonia was influenced by this powerful energy.

Several years ago, my family took our annual vacation and rented a country farmhouse high on top of a ridge. A few days after we arrived, Patrick rented a couple of old, rickety bicycles to tool around on. Not surprisingly, Sonia, who was nine years old at the time, wanted to ride one. Unsure whether it would be safe because the road was so steep, I asked Patrick if he thought it was wise to let her.

"I think it will be fine," he reassured me. "I'll go with her, and we'll only ride to the bottom of the hill."

And so, as I urged them to be careful and told them I'd pick them up in 30 minutes, they strapped on helmets and set off.

After the half hour passed, I jumped in the car and sped down the road just in time to see Sonia awkwardly pedaling behind Patrick, obviously having the time of her life.

I was happy to see that she was managing so well on such an old, oversized rattletrap and congratulated her: "Good job, Sonia! Now let's put the bike in the car, and I'll give you a lift back to the house."

"But Mom," she protested, "I don't want to *drive* up! I'd rather ride."

"Sonia, it's a three-mile rise!" I shot back. "It's very hard for even an expert cyclist like your dad to go up that hill. You can't possibly make it!"

"You don't know that!" she argued even more energetically. "I want to try!" She had a point. I didn't *think* that she could do it but, in fact, I didn't *know* for sure.

"Please let me!" she persisted.

Patrick and I exchanged glances, and he shrugged as if to say, "It's up to you."

"Okay, Sonia, I'll tell you what. Ride as far as you can, and I'll drive the car behind you. When you feel like you can't go any farther, pull over and I'll take you the rest of the way."

"Great!" she yelled, already heading up the incline.

I followed her closely as she pedaled steadily after her father, sandwiching her protectively between us.

As I watched her, my eyes grew wide with disbelief. She was keeping up with Patrick and not faltering for even a moment.

They got to the top of the first slope and began climbing the second without hesitation. Soon they arrived at its crest and slowly inched up the third. I expected Patrick, who had cycled for years, to have no problem, but I was amazed by how Sonia, struggling just to reach the pedals, maintained his pace.

Finally they topped the last hill and coasted victoriously into the farmhouse yard. Much to my astonishment, Sonia had done it! She'd ridden up a three-mile vertical rise without missing a beat!

She ripped off her helmet and ran joyously toward me. "Wow! Mom, I did it! Surprised?"

"You bet I am!" I exclaimed. "However did you manage that?"

Beaming with pride, she answered, "Easy. I imagined that Daddy was pulling me and that you were pushing me, and I just rode along in the middle!"

One of the most profound things you can do as a parent to awaken your children's desire to reach for their own natural highest potential is to give them your full awareness and attention and witness their efforts. This doesn't mean hovering over them, projecting your every fear and being a control freak. Nor do you have to abandon your own path. You simply need to be conscious of them as individuals and pay attention in order to help spark their interest in discovering for themselves who they are and what great things they can achieve.

Presence Provides Protection

The importance of really being present for your children can't be overemphasized. I once worked with Detective J. J. Bittenbinder, who had a TV series called *Tough Target*. We both are adamant that awareness and paying attention are the keys to personal safety.

I take it a step further. I believe that criminals are very intuitive in their own way, because as predators, they "sniff out" their victims by noticing who isn't paying attention and is therefore vulnerable. If you're preoccupied, in a relentless hurry, and rarely (if ever) truly aware of your children, they'll emanate an aura of vulnerability that the "bad guys" can sense.

I discovered this as a child of 12, with my two girlfriends, Jane and Deborah. Both Deborah's mom and mine were very attentive, always checking on us and making us report in to them every so often when we played outside. Jane often complained bitterly about our restrictions because they cramped her style. Her own mother was a single parent who worked at a dry cleaner's all day. And as Jane proudly said, "She lets me do whatever I want."

One day, the three of us were hanging out in front of my house when a car pulled up and a man who looked about 40 years old leaned out the window and beckoned.

"Hey, you!" he called, pointing to Jane. "Come here a minute. I'd like to talk to you."

She walked over, and he asked her if she wanted to be a model. He handed her a business card and told her that he worked for an agency. He also said that she was prettier than Deborah and I and that he wanted to sign her on. Needless to say, Jane was incredibly flattered.

"I'd love to model," she answered breathlessly, "but first I have to ask my mother."

Then she ran over to us and very excitedly said, "I have to go, you guys. That man's from a modeling agency, and he wants to hire me! I can't believe it! I'll see you later. I'm going to call my mom and tell her the great news." Then she was off, racing home before we had time to ask a single question. We watched as the man in the car followed her, feeling jealous and left out.

We waited patiently for her to return and give us all the details, but after a while, when she didn't come back, Deborah and I got nervous. I told my mother what had happened, and she phoned Jane's house. When nobody answered, she immediately called Jane's mom at work, who was horrified when she heard that her daughter had taken off alone with a stranger following her. She contacted the police right away, and a search began, but Jane was nowhere to be found.

We were all worried sick, especially Deborah and me. My friend and I were also thinking how lucky we were that the man hadn't gone after us, too.

Later that evening, Jane was found, naked and disoriented, wandering alone in the mountains. Apparently the "modeling agent" had convinced her to get into his car, and then drove her to an isolated area, where he forced her to undress and photographed her in the nude. Then he molested her and left her there. Luckily, she hadn't been raped or murdered as well, but the criminal was never caught.

Knowing more now than I did then, it's not surprising to me that the man didn't beckon to Deborah or me. I'm sure he sensed the difference in the parental presence surrounding us. As Deborah said, "I wouldn't have even asked my mom. I was sure what the answer would be!" It was as though the man had intuitively known which of us was the most vulnerable and easiest to prey upon.

Tune In, Not Out

Paying attention and being aware are fundamental to living a six-sensory life. Your children start out with this natural, intense presence of mind, but eventually they're encouraged to tune it out. The world will try to teach them to ignore their inner guidance soon enough, but don't let them learn it from you. Emphasize the importance of awareness through your own example and how you treat them. Meditate, and be interested and tuned in to your kids and your partner (if you have one). You may have to fight for the time you need to center and ground yourself instead of getting swept away by the endless to-do lists of life, but it's essential for everyone's well-being.

Start right now by doing what I did on the porch that day I described earlier. Take in a big, long, luxurious breath and return to the present. Realize that all you have is this moment and refuse to let your ruminations about yesterday—or your fears and anxieties about tomorrow—steal it.

Establishing New Habits

When you're overworked and buried in tasks with no time to do them, you'll find it very hard to be patient with anything, let alone with your children. Parenting these days is a full-time job that most of us juggle on top of our demanding careers and other obligations, leaving us stressed, strained, and moving in hyper-drive. This is precisely the time to do the following exercise.

— **A present for you.** You can do this exercise sitting down or standing up, with your eyes closed. Place both feet flat on the ground or floor and let out a long, slow exhale. Imagine everything that's bothering you draining out of your body and into the ground through the soles of your feet. Then, very slowly, place your left hand over your heart and your right hand over your belly. Take in a full, luxurious breath while saying silently to yourself: *I am present.* Repeat this affirmation as you breathe out.

Do this five times whenever you feel overwhelmed or in need of space. Avoid the tendency to rush through this exercise, even if you feel you must. Doing the entire process at a *very* leisurely pace only requires four minutes at most, and will expand your sense of time. Taking a few moments to quiet your nervous system and nurture yourself can save you hours of fruitless anxiety, sudden blowups, potential confrontations, and costly oversights. This brief centering technique will also alleviate pressure and allow you to engage with your children in a more loving and peaceful way.

— **Take 20.** Allow yourself 20 minutes every day just to be with your child (or children)—playing, talking, and listening to them. You can divide this time into two 10-minute segments, one in the morning and one in the evening, but try to set aside 20 minutes altogether.

— **Expand your awareness.** You can develop your ability to pay attention just by taking small steps. Even little changes can help you deepen your intuitive skills. Try this!

Today:

- Notice one new thing about your children.

- Take a moment to look at your partner from a fresh angle and see something different.

- Observe some aspect of your neighborhood that has never caught your attention before.

This week:

- Discover something unfamiliar at work.

- Notice one new quality about yourself.

- Identify how you waste your time and ask yourself what you can do to change this. Also ask yourself if you're *willing* to do so.

— **Creating deeper family connections.** You can become more present to your spouse and children by following these suggestions:

1. When you leave work, *leave work.*

2. Go for a walk with your child, holding hands if possible.

3. Enjoy a family meal (preferably home cooked) with everyone present a minimum of once a week.

4. Have a story time after dinner at least once a month. Share memories and anecdotes from your own childhood and your parents'. Let your children ask questions, and follow their line of curiosity.

5. Don't answer the phone during dinner.

6. Say no to work-related calls in the evenings and on weekends (or at least during the hours designated for family).

7. Make up a bedtime story to tell your children.

8. Set aside one day a week to rest, relax, and connect with one another.

9. Do projects with your kids, such as:

   - Planting a garden
   - Working in the yard
   - Painting their room

- Decorating cookies
- Baking a pie

10. Avoid using television as a substitute for true together time, and have real conversations instead.

Reflections

- What was your most recent high-quality experience with your children? With your partner (or with a good friend, if you're a single parent)? With your parent(s)? With yourself? Is it difficult for you to make room in your schedule and be fully present for your loved ones? If so, what do you fear?

- Name your three favorite ways to spend quality time with your kids and spouse (or a close friend if you're single). Ask them to do the same.

- What differences (if any) have you noticed or experienced in the energy of your family since you've improved your ability to be conscious with them?

- What (if anything) have you eliminated from your life to increase your awareness of in the moment? What do you still need to do?

- Have you noticed any shifts in your children since you've becoming more attentive to them? Have they mentioned any changes?

- How do you feel about being more present for yourself? For your kids?

- Have you had any new intuitive insights regarding your family since you've started to pay greater attention? If so, what are they?

Reminders

- Are you meditating regularly? What, if any, differences has it made in your consciousness?

- Have you practiced the thumb-forefinger stress buster? Are you staying aware in the moment?

One of the ways in which you can expand your capacity to be present for yourself and your family is to practice listening to your heart. We'll explore how to tune in to its messages in the next chapter.

Chapter Three

THE HEART OF THE MATTER

When my mother was a young woman, she suffered a severe case of rheumatic fever that caused her to gradually lose her hearing in both ears. By the time I was born, the loss was pronounced, so I grew up with a mom who was nearly deaf. She took it all in stride and used to tell us, "It's not a problem for me because Divine Spirit gives us two ways to listen—with our ears and, more important, with our heart." In my family, the second approach was emphasized. "It's interesting," my mother would say, "that when you use your heart, your ears work better, too."

My mom's lesson gave us a six-sensory perspective from our earliest years. It influenced how we took in information and helped us become aware of not only the *content* of a message, but its *intent* or essence as well. I learned to listen from my heart both by noticing how my mother tuned in to her own inner guidance, and by experiencing her great attention to what *I* had to say. Although she struggled at times to discern my words, I always knew that she was keenly interested in understanding me. In short, I felt heard.

Sometimes when we talked to my mom, she closed her eyes and energetically sensed our communication. Her heart-based orientation opened a pathway between all my family members—one that conveyed connection and meaning that mere speech failed to register. This channel was open even when we said nothing . . . it was as though our dialogue had moved up an octave and we conversed on a purer, telepathic level.

Inner knowing is actually the art and practice of listening with the heart, for that's where the voice of higher wisdom speaks. I believe that we all start out in life attuned to this source. Just reflect on kids' acute perception and natural ability to absorb whatever comes their way—both content and intent—in its entirety. They pick up absolutely everything that's "in the air." In fact, I've seen them register the truth of a situation, whether good or bad, faster than the adults around them. And babies naturally relax around people who are at ease with them, while they fuss or scream at those who may smile and coo but are really uncomfortable or afraid. Infants feel the difference in their hearts.

I recall that when I was about five years old, I came home from kindergarten one day and was filled with a strong sense of dread and sadness. I worried and wondered what was wrong. Even though there were no obvious signs of trouble, my heart felt something wasn't quite right.

That evening, my grandmother, who lived with us, had a stroke in the backyard. I'll never forget that when the ambulance came to get her, I wasn't surprised. I'd felt that something was about to happen, even though I wasn't sure what! Now I realized that it was about Grandma. I don't know whether she or my parents were aware that she was ill, or if her stroke was a shock for them, but I do know that my vibes had warned me.

Our inner source of wisdom is centered in the heart and offers us a broader, deeper perspective and understanding. It brings our attention to the unseen, subtle aspects of life and directs us toward a more creative, loving, and insightful approach to difficulties.

We all feel heart-based connections from time to time because it's our nature to do so. The problems arise when we tune out or doubt this awareness and surrender to the world of outside appearances and opinions instead.

Many people fear having a point of view that's different from others'. Therefore, even when their heart gives them clear guidance, they'll often discount or ignore its message. For example, my husband used to amuse himself by playing a goofy game he made up called "10:15." When Patrick went to parties, he'd ask other guests, "What time do you have?" No matter what they answered, he'd reply, "That's funny . . . my watch says it's 10:15." Then he'd observe how many of them would question the accuracy of their own watches before doubting his. Sometimes the number was as high as 80 percent! It just goes to show how easily we can be thrown into uncertainty, believing that someone else knows better.

Children are especially vulnerable to losing their faith in themselves unless you teach them otherwise. They need to learn from *you* that it's important to tune in to and trust their inner guidance and not be afraid to express what they feel—even if it contradicts what others tell them. When you show kids how to listen to their hearts and honor what they know, you affirm their intuition.

My daughter Sabrina is a naturally spontaneous girl when it comes to following her vibes because we've always encouraged her to do so. She never hesitates to communicate her feelings. When she was only three years old, she attended preschool; and one time when I went to pick her up, her teacher shared this story about what had happened that day: Ms. Agnes thought that her young students were being difficult and unruly, and she was having a hard time being patient with them. Finally, she sent the entire class to the corner to take a "time-out." There they sat, hanging their heads in shame for several minutes, when suddenly Sabrina whispered something to them. They all nodded in silent, enthusiastic agreement.

A moment later, Sabrina stood up, very gently tiptoed over to the teacher's desk, and quietly said, "Ms. Agnes, I'm worried about you. We're all feeling fine in the corner. Would you like to sit with us over there until you feel better, too?"

Sabrina smiled meekly and then tiptoed back to her corner and sat down once again. Her teacher burst out laughing, feeling as though she'd been caught. She ended the children's time-out and took a break herself.

Ms. Agnes told me that the truth was that the kids hadn't misbehaved more than usual. In fact, *she* was the one who had been out of balance. She'd had a big disagreement with her husband that morning and was still agitated when she arrived at school. In spite of her efforts to get on with the day, the argument continued to bother her and made her very cranky. She admitted that Sabrina had been right in sensing that it was her teacher who needed to feel better and that the preschoolers weren't the problem. She also said that she admired Sabrina's awareness and courage in expressing herself.

It's important to understand that children naturally listen with their hearts. As parents, we need to follow their good example and affirm for them how intuitive this is, even if the rest of the world has forgotten how to do so.

If kids aren't censured or subjected to an environment in which inner awareness is discouraged—and if they're allowed to feel and freely share their deepest emotions—they'll establish an extremely solid connection to their higher wisdom. They'll remain conscious of the vital messages of their sixth sense and look to their hearts for verification.

It Begins with Listening

Learning to listen with the heart begins with training yourself to focus on what someone's trying to communicate. I recently tuned in to a radio program that reported that most people hear only 50 percent of what's said, and retain just 20 percent of that information for more than an hour. I wonder what percentage of true attention parents have available for their children.

Real listening means just that—it's not interrupting, fixing, solving, cutting off, or shutting down your kids before they fully express what they have to say. Don't let impatience cause you to start speaking before they're finished, for the great majority of all problems in relationships (including the one with your own intuition) stem from someone's feeling of not being heard.

When your children are upset or angry, or simply need to share something with you, practice giving them your full attention. If they're squabbling with their siblings, listen to each individual, one at a time. Make a rule in your home that when people are mad or need to speak, they can talk about everything that's bothering them, without censorship or interruption, on the condition that they use a calm tone of voice. They shouldn't be allowed to scream or insult anyone while expressing their problem. This doesn't mean that you must always agree with what they say, but you do need to care enough to allow your children to openly communicate their feelings.

I realize that it can be very hard to listen sometimes, especially if you're overtired or in a hurry. Unfortunately, these are usually the moments your kids will approach you. Because it's often inconvenient or even impossible to truly pay attention when you're feeling harried, agree with them in advance on a regular time—perhaps just before bed—when you'll actively concentrate on what they want to tell you. Then honor that commitment. Pick the best and most realistic time of day, when you can be completely present and won't be uninterrupted.

Establishing this routine takes great effort and patience, but it's highly worthwhile and is a terrific catalyst for awakening intuition. In order to become balanced and grounded, we all need to get in touch with and express our feelings—including anger—and be *heard*. This ritual will clear the air, keep you attuned to your inner voice and your kids' true needs, and help build the basis for a solid relationship with your own "Inner Teacher."

Be Honest

Having an open heart is central to intuitive awareness, and none is more receptive than a child's. Our job as parents is to protect their natural gift by having open hearts ourselves. To help our kids believe in themselves and not doubt what they feel, we first need to develop our self-confidence and faith in our vibes. We can lead them to find the courage to stick to what's true for them and to not ignore their inner guidance by modeling these behaviors ourselves. One way we can do so is by being completely honest and sharing our feelings truthfully.

I once had a client named Martin who came for a reading at his wife's suggestion because he was quite frustrated about his relationship with his daughter. Martin was extremely intellectual and intensely uncomfortable with any outward expression of emotion. He strove to keep himself on an even keel at all times and did everything in his power to make his world pleasant—no matter what. He thought that by accomplishing this, he was creating a loving environment, but in fact, he was exercising control.

In his quest to avoid any negativity, he found that he was alienating his five-year-old daughter, Gloria. She disregarded him most of the time, often speaking to him rudely and making it clear that she preferred the company of Mommy. And she loved to make a scene.

He said to me, "I don't get it, Sonia. Gloria and her mother fight constantly, yet when I show up and am friendly, she's contemptuous. She has no respect for me at all, and it's upsetting me. I try not to let it show, but it's not working."

It was true that Gloria didn't have much respect for her father, but she had a good reason: She was very intuitive and instinctively knew that her dad's superficial "All is well" approach to life was phony. The picture he painted for her wasn't coming from his heart, and she felt it. She could sense that by avoiding confrontation, he was also rejecting passion, energy, and maybe life itself . . . and that included her. At least her mother was real, even though she got angry sometimes; and that made Gloria feel safe.

But she was a little girl and didn't have an intellectual understanding of all this. She only knew that her father bothered her. She was simply expressing what her instincts told her and was declaring: "I know the real story, and you can't fool me!"

Martin needed to be more authentic with Gloria and express what was in his heart, which at times would mean showing irritation, enforcing discipline, and setting limits with her. As he became more open and shared his feelings more honestly, his daughter did come to feel safer and more comfortable with him.

In a similar vein, my client Mary Ann came to see me a while ago because her 17-year-old son, Ryan, had just been arrested for marijuana possession. She was appalled and told me, "Sonia, we've provided him with an ideal home life. I just don't understand it!"

"But Mary Ann," I responded, "I don't see such a model environment. You and your husband are completely estranged and barely acknowledge one another."

"Maybe so, but Ryan doesn't know that," she said.

"Oh, really? How could he not be aware of it?"

"We've decided to keep our marital issues to ourselves because we don't want to upset him while he's in high school. We'll deal with them when he leaves for college."

"So you live in two separate worlds without acknowledging it?" I continued.

"Yes," she replied. "I have my horses, and my husband has his work. We don't talk a lot, but we're always pleasant with each other when we do."

"Has Ryan ever asked about your problems?" I probed gently.

"Once, months ago, but we reassured him that we were working things out and doing fine. He forgot all about it after that."

"Well, from what I can tell, he hasn't forgotten about it at all. Quite the opposite," I said. "He intuitively feels *everything*. He has simply decided that since you two have created a house of denial and shut down your hearts, each escaping into your own activities, why shouldn't he do the same thing?"

"What do you mean?" she asked.

"I mean that Ryan has done what you've done. He has fallen out of touch with his heart and set up a world of appearances—just like his parents. After all, if you two aren't truthful and aren't really there, why should *he* try to stay present? He just chose marijuana as his distraction of choice. Unfortunately, it's illegal; and he got caught."

To say that Mary Ann was surprised by my perspective would be putting it mildly. After Ryan was placed on probation, I suggested that they all get counseling and urged them to make a sincere attempt to get to the heart of the matter and speak truthfully with one another.

Mary Ann called six months later to tell me that she and her husband were separating and that Ryan was preparing to leave for college. All three of them had "come clean" (so to speak) after months of intense family therapy. "We're going through hard times with so much change, but our relationships are more honest, which I think makes Ryan feel more secure. At least he isn't stoned anymore," she reported.

The Family Meeting

My family has a weekly gathering where everyone shares their deepest emotions and thoughts. This ritual, perhaps more than any other, has assisted us in opening our hearts and connecting with our intuition. Our meetings are held after dinner on Sunday evenings and usually last from 15 minutes to an hour. Each of us takes a turn to "check in," which consists of expressing how we feel, saying what (if anything) is troubling or challenging us, and explaining what kind of help we need from other family members. It's a time of honesty, clarity, support, and receiving that allows us to connect with our own awareness and to one another. Our talks create goodwill and safety among us, as well as preventing misunderstandings from piling up. They also establish the habit of authentic communication at home.

As parents, you can do a lot to awaken your children's intuition by turning to the heart. Recognize and acknowledge what's real—both seen and unseen—and encourage your kids to do the same. After all, they can sense the truth, and you need to affirm it, too.

As you work to help your children awaken their intuition, realize that this doesn't mean that you want them to focus on some "otherworldly" place or phenomenon or pursue messages from outer space. It's quite the opposite: Inner awareness is about paying attention to what you experience and developing a keen sense of how energy (both seen and unseen) affects you and others. Truly heightened perception is the understanding that comes from recognizing that we're all spiritual beings who are connected to one another and share the same breath.

In order to connect to our six-sensory awareness, we must turn inward and look for the truth in our hearts, where our true self or soul resides. It's only when we listen with both our heads and our hearts—and express what we feel to be true—that we'll receive clear and complete guidance.

This way of listening is the very foundation of intuitive living. When we go within, we tap into an unlimited source of higher intelligence and direction, for our hearts are wells of insight, bright ideas, and solutions. It's there that we become aware of the subtle, hidden aspects of life and, so often, the truth about whatever we're facing.

Tools for Tuning In to Your Heart

Listening to this voice of the soul requires practice, and it may take several weeks of concentrated effort to get into the habit of tuning in to your heart for direction. Here are several tools to help you begin:

Listening to Your Heart

Every time you need guidance—or simply reassurance—close your eyes; take a few deep, cleansing breaths; and place your attention directly on your heart. Allow your focus to rest there quietly for a moment or two, and then ask your heart to lead you. Trust whatever feelings come up, and don't censor or discount anything. If you don't receive a response immediately, don't worry. Just relax and remain open and patient. Before you know it, you'll receive its message.

Breathing as You Listen

My teachers taught me that it's much easier to tune in to your heart and fully listen to others when you take complete breaths. So often, miscommunication occurs because everyone is neglecting to exhale, making it almost impossible to truly hear anything. Whenever you want to deliver a heartfelt communication or get in touch with what's in your own heart, begin by taking three or four deep, cleansing breaths; and then return to a calm, steady rhythm of inhalation and exhalation.

Put Your Hand Over Your Heart

One of my family's favorite techniques is actually placing one of our hands over our hearts, letting it rest there as we speak and listen to each another. This is our signal that we have something important to say and want to be truly heard. It's an especially effective method for settling arguments and opening up troubled communications.

Reflections

- Was anyone in your childhood home available to give you their full attention? When?

- Were you ever conscious of the difference between listening with the heart and not doing so?

- Were you able to freely express your innermost feelings as you were growing up, or was it forbidden in your family?

- If you were censored as a kid, are you still stopping yourself from openly sharing your thoughts and emotions?

Reminders

- Have you used the Put-Your-Hand-Over-Your-Heart technique? What results did you have?

- Have you tried the Breathing-as-You-Listen exercise? What was the outcome?

- Have you held a family meeting? What was your experience?

- Is your heart opening? If so, how does it feel? Have your loved ones noticed?

- What (if any) shifts has the Listening-to-Your-Heart tool brought about in your home?

Chapter Four

CREATING A SPIRITUALLY GROUNDED HOME

Once you begin raising your awareness and opening your heart, it's important to examine the energy and atmosphere of your home to ensure that it also encourages intuitive expression and provides spiritual safety to both you and your children.

A few years ago, during the extremely frustrating renovation of our very first house, Patrick and I were having a great deal of difficulty getting along. We were both trying our best to handle the stress, but the construction was moving too slowly, the costs were soaring out of sight, the workmen weren't doing their jobs as well as we wanted them to, and the disruption left us nowhere to go to recover our equilibrium. Every day brought new disagreements, each more serious than the last; and due to the cumulative pressure, we were soon at war.

Tension seemed to hang in the air, and it got to the point where we'd be in perfectly fine spirits until we entered the front door, when we'd instantly fall into a cross mood. We were all absolutely miserable—not only Patrick and me, but the girls as well.

During this distressing period, Sabrina, who was two years old at the time, cried, screamed, hollered, and threw a fit every evening as soon as we went to bed. Often, no matter what we did, she wouldn't sleep through the night. It finally occurred to me that she was trying to get our attention. Through her tantrums, she was struggling to tell us how much the toxic energy of the house was bothering her; and the only time she could get us to notice her was at midnight, when everything else settled down.

Sabrina was right: Our home *had* taken on a very bleak atmosphere. It had become so stressful and chaotic that it failed to provide any of us with the essentials: safety, serenity, and protection from the world. The negative energy caused all of us to feel volatile, threatened, and defensive. Our house wasn't a haven to retreat *to,* but a place to retreat *from*. We needed to do something immediately. This was an emergency!

Patrick and I called a truce and discussed the need to create a sanctuary in the midst of the crisis. We decided to concentrate our renovation efforts on the bedrooms and finish them up as quickly as possible so that at least we would have somewhere to go for peace and quiet. This important decision made a tremendous difference in the way we were all feeling. Having restored a little harmony, we were able to relax and regain our perspective. Even the girls seemed to calm down a bit once they were in their own completed rooms.

It's interesting to me now to remember how obsessed Patrick and I were with removing all the toxic materials in that house so that our daughters would be safe. We stripped the lead paint, removed the asbestos, and pulled out all the flammable wiring. But in focusing so intently on the potential physical dangers, we failed to consider the nonphysical hazardous conditions. The disrupted atmosphere was just as poisonous as asbestos or lead. Arguing, disorder, stress, and change filled our home with a feeling of great dis-ease.

It took a lot of effort on our part, but eventually we were able to turn the situation around. Very intentionally, we began to bless the rooms and ask the Universe to restore tranquility. We also methodically played beautiful music during the day to raise the vibration. We maintained as much order as was possible in a construction zone, and after several months, the atmosphere in the house started to improve as we created a clearer and more peaceful energy. What a relief!

With the return to calm, the kids settled down. Sabrina, who'd had frequent nightmares and been restless at night, began to sleep easily from bedtime until morning. In addition, Sonia's sensitive outbursts simmered down. Patrick and I restored goodwill between us and started enjoying each other again. Finally, the renovation was finished, and there was no doubt about it: Having a peaceful home made a huge difference in all of our lives, and we were now committed to maintaining it.

Energy and Place

The experience with our home made me very aware of how important the environment we live in actually is. Just as people have certain vibrations, so do places. For example, the energy of a church or synagogue is vastly different from a subway station's. Even the atmosphere in one house of worship may vary greatly from that of another.

All day long, we're subjected to many kinds of energy that we can't control, and this is especially true for kids. Their classrooms, school buses, day-care centers, and even their after-school jobs have specific vibrations. Additionally, in many divorced families, a lot of young people spend time both at Mom's house, which has one kind of atmosphere, and at Dad's, which has another. Every one of these places has an energetic field that influences children.

Ask yourself what kind of energy your home has. Is it a calm and tranquil place? Do your kids feel safe and protected from the world there? Is it peaceful? Is it clean and organized? When they come in the door, can they let their guard down and feel secure? Are they able to open up their awareness and expand into reverie and imagination in relatively relaxed conditions? Or do they have to hunker down, run for cover, and walk on eggshells?

Sacred Space

I've experienced an enormous variety of vibrations in homes, both in the course of my work as an intuitive and in pursuing my hobby of exploring old houses. What I've seen tells me that many,

many people are unaware of how energy affects them and have no idea how much they need to create a sacred space to dwell in, both for themselves and for their children.

I'm truly alarmed to see just how many individuals live in the intuitive equivalent of a toxic-waste dump. We have to recognize that this shouldn't be acceptable, because we—and especially our kids—are sensitive beings. We have just as great a need for peace and tranquility as any other delicate creature. We should therefore commit ourselves to creating a sacred space for ourselves and our families.

I was first introduced to the power of spiritually grounded environments while studying with my teacher Dr. Trenton Tully as a teenager. He gave lessons in metaphysics and spirituality in a magnificent old mansion in Denver. When I first walked through the front door of that lovely building, I was immediately taken with the wafting scent of incense, the beauty of the architecture and furniture, the glow of the candles, and—most of all—the realization that I was in a very special, holy place. The aura was as clear as a summer sunrise, and the energy was as calm as the still waters on a lake at dusk. The atmosphere was soothing and made me feel completely safe, as though I were in a refuge where nothing could harm me.

Dr. Tully told me that the mansion itself was very healing because of all the intention that had been directed toward making it that way. He emphasized the need to create serenity in order to grow spiritually and awaken intuition. "It's very hard to be aware," he'd say, "if you find yourself constantly subjected to confusing and disruptive forces. Strive, therefore, to create and live in calm and harmonious energy."

The first and most obvious step to create a peaceful sacred space in a home is to keep it clean, organized, and filled with objects that comfort the spirit. Dr. Tully taught me that everything is comprised of energy and that all of our possessions take on our vibrations. We can feel this in Grandpa's chair, Aunt Mary's shawl, Dad's gold watch, or our own favorite childhood toy. The affection that we have for cherished belongings is especially absorbed by them and can be sensed.

The same holds true for negative energy. If our family is living in messy, neglected disarray, we'll come to resent it. This emotion will then emanate and become palpable in our home, further compounding the toxicity. The best cure for this problem is to clean and clear away everything that isn't necessary or used, or which doesn't bring us comfort. If something is ugly, irritating, broken, or useless, get rid of it!

Clean Up, Clear Out

I made a trip to see my friend Lois, a veteran pack rat, a few years ago. When I arrived, I found her house deluged with unloved, outgrown toys; furniture; and junk. She had three children between the ages of 4 and 11 who seemed to have absolutely no interest in the mountain of stuff lying about, maneuvering around it as though it were a maze.

During my visit, however, I noticed that they did have to endure Mom's demands to "Clean up this place!" several times a day. The atmosphere was cramped, uncomfortable, and extremely unpleasant, and everyone in the house *felt* it.

The effort it took to navigate around the place kept the kids and their mother from putting their attention on more interesting matters—like each other. And the mutual irritation and resentment everyone was feeling hung in the air like a cloud.

If Lois simply cleared out the unwanted things (and energy), it would really make a difference in lightening up the atmosphere in their home. I made this suggestion on my way to the airport, as she was once again apologizing for everyone's bad manners. She'd considered doing this before but hadn't. "I know you're right, Sonia," she said. "I don't understand why I haven't gotten rid of the junk. Just lazy, perhaps."

"Well, it would help raise the energy in your home to a more pleasant level if you did. Why don't you start by donating the things you no longer find interesting to people who could use them?"

"That's a novel idea!" she exclaimed.

I visited Lois a year later. This time the house was clear of clutter, and the vibration felt much more peaceful. As I walked in, my friend said, "Sonia, we took your advice and cleaned out everything we didn't use and gave it to the Salvation Army. Our rule now is that for every new item that comes in, an old one goes out. The energy around here feels a lot better, don't you think?"

"Absolutely!" I answered, feeling relieved myself.

Lois's idea of keeping things moving was an excellent way to clear away negative vibrations and restore tranquility, and I suggest it to my clients and students all the time. Try it, because it definitely works!

Play Areas, Peaceful Areas

Another technique for creating a peaceful aura in your home is to designate some areas for play and disorder, leaving the other rooms for quiet and calm. If you don't have much space to implement this plan, you can set aside certain *times* for recreation and others for tranquility and repose.

In our house, the girls are allowed to make messes and do projects in the basement, but the bedrooms are kept orderly and serene. This doesn't prevent the girls from being creative in their rooms—they just have to keep them clean so that they can sleep in peaceful energy.

I'm sure that every parent of an adolescent is groaning about my suggestion. However, the idea here is to teach your kids that disruption and chaos diminish *their* energy and awareness. I advise my teenage clients to become conscious of how the vibrations of a place affect them. Clear, orderly spaces have a soothing quality, while messy ones are draining and upsetting. The key is to help teenagers create their own system of organization and ask them how you can help. Do they need drawers, shelves, or a desk? Can you provide these?

Establishing New Habits

— **Creating a sacred altar.** A wonderful way to enhance the healing vibration of a home is to create a sacred altar. It should be set up where it will be safe . . . on a table, a small box, or even on the floor if no one will disturb it there. On your altar, place beloved objects, photos, and talismans representing the people and things you love. These may include religious icons, family photos, and articles from nature (such as shells or stones)—anything that lifts your spirits and moves you into your heart. You may also want to use fresh flowers, candles, or incense.

Let the altar serve as a site for contemplation, reverie, meditation, and prayer. It will become charged with the alchemy of peace and tranquility and serve as a place of healing in your home. A personal altar is usually so compelling that once children see it, they'll want to contribute to it or set up one themselves.

— **Music and flower-essence aromatherapy.** Another lovely technique for generating soothing energy in the home is by playing relaxing, meditation, or classical music. It's well known that Baroque pieces such as those by Bach, Vivaldi, Telemann, or Handel calm listeners' heartbeats and create an inner state of tranquility. It's a terrific antidote to some of the more dissonant experiences you have during the day.

You can also cultivate a healing atmosphere by using aromatherapy to fill your home with the fragrance of essential oils that make you feel serene and at ease—such as lavender, chamomile, and rose. You simply put a drop or two of your favorite oil on a lightbulb ring (available where essential oils are sold) in each room. The warmth of the bulb diffuses the oil, permeating the air with a beautiful scent and energy. Aromatherapy works directly on the nervous system to help you relax.

— **A tranquility room.** Another great way to create healing energy in your home is by designating one room as a sanctuary where no one is ever allowed to argue or even enter in an angry mood. If you live in a small apartment or have little space, then pick the bathroom. It's a natural choice anyway. I've had hundreds of adults tell me that when they were kids, they used to hide there when arguments broke out or they needed some privacy. It worked so well that they still do so.

— **Put living things in every room.** By placing some of nature's gifts throughout your home, you'll create a healing atmosphere. You can use potted and flowering plants; or pets such as fish, birds, turtles, hamsters, or gerbils. The point is to create an environment that hosts the beauty and energy of the natural world. Both animals and plants have very high, pure vibrations and will help clear out sadness, grief, anger, and depression. They'll also fill your place with love and light.

Of course I'm not suggesting that you get too many pets or let your house become a jungle! This goes back to my first dictum: order. Take on only what you can care for, because dying plants and ailing animals will produce the opposite of the energy you want.

Be Sensitive

A home whose vibration is safe, healing, and gentle is free of addiction, chronic rage, dishonesty, fear, and abuse. I've seen so many joyous and delightful children who are bright, creative, and keenly intuitive languish and wither in households where dysfunction, stress, and terror are the name of the game. As parents, we're required to take a look in the mirror and ask ourselves if we're doing our best to provide our kids with a protective and spiritually grounded environment.

I can't count the number of wounded clients I've counseled who've come to me to recover the loss of safety and inner awareness they suffered in their childhood. These are the adult children of alcoholics, rage-aholics, and workaholics who ignored the psychic atmosphere in their homes—or worse yet, made it toxic. I've seen many people in despair, not knowing what or whom to believe because they grew up in chaos and couldn't count on anyone. Without trust, we can't connect to our higher wisdom and awaken our intuition.

More than any other factor, the environment in which kids live determines whether they'll open their hearts, follow their truth, and be themselves in life . . . or if they'll simply become "actors" who take on a superficial guise designed to protect them from the tumult and abuse they endure in their own homes.

Be Fair

Children are so vulnerable and dependent on adults that it's easy not to give them a vote on what happens to them. It's also tempting to ignore how our own problems affect them. But just because we don't tell our kids that we're having trouble doesn't mean that they don't *feel* it. They do, and it scares them because they usually can't do anything about it.

The best way to create a safe and sacred home isn't to eliminate family problems. That's impossible anyway because life is full of challenges. Instead, have the integrity and fairness of heart to communicate with your children when issues do arise, and let them know that *they* are not to blame.

Don't hide the truth or, worse yet, use your kids as scapegoats when difficulties come up. This will only confuse them because they intuitively feel everything. Unfortunately, they may not always correctly interpret their vibes. If you're troubled but won't acknowledge it or seek help, they'll assume that it's their fault and take on guilt and shame.

I had a client who was divorcing his wife after a three-year cold war. Although they were barely civil to each other, they never discussed their problems with their four- and eight-year-old. The kids felt the tension in the air so intensely that one developed anxiety attacks, while the other took to chewing his fingernails down to the quick.

My client finally moved out but didn't fully explain to the children why he and their mom had separated. He told me that his kids were emotionally devastated and no longer trusted him, themselves, or anyone else, and he couldn't figure out why.

"I was only trying to protect them," he said. "Why would they want to know about my issues with their mother?"

But he wasn't actually helping them—he was only avoiding what made him uncomfortable. The family is now sorting itself out in counseling, but they have a long way to go.

If your household is tense, uptight, unhappy, toxic, angry, unsafe, or insecure, ask yourself why. And more important, question why you're willing to accept such a disabling condition for yourself and your children. If you've been avoiding doing the work of finding your own peace, now is the time to begin. For the sake of both you and your kids, start looking for solutions.

If you have addictions or marital problems or are in a spiritual crisis, seek help. And if you're lonely, exhausted, overextended, or isolated, be gentle with yourself . . . and <u>seek help.</u>

Part of the difficulty of parenting today is that the work it involves—on top of the demands of a full-time job—leaves you little time to nurture yourself as an individual. And when your own spirit is neglected, everyone else feels it and suffers, too. By making room in your life for friendships, community, and other means of support, you'll feel renewed and have more energy for your family.

Remember to be fair with your kids and let them know the real source of your trouble. Don't let them become scapegoats or expect them to parent you. It isn't fair, and it will shut down their open hearts. If you've already fallen into this trap, apologize. They'll appreciate it.

As you work on this, you may find it helpful to attend a church, see a counselor, visit a friend, or join a creativity or exercise class. Go to God in prayer or stand before a mirror to find the self-love and integrity to do *whatever* it takes to create the peace *you* need and deserve so that your children will grow up in a home that provides them with the sacred space and protection from the world that *they* deserve.

It's profoundly disabling to our souls when we live in an atmosphere of relentlessly toxic, negative, stressed, angry, disruptive energy. It wears us out, makes us sick, desensitizes our kids, and disconnects us from our spiritual center. It also shuts down our awareness and cuts off our capacity to feel and follow our inner wisdom.

In America, this problem is epidemic; and as parents, we need to shake off the tendency to accept such noxious conditions—both for ourselves and for our children. We'd never consider living in a poisonous physical environment, yet we accept the harmful energy that surrounds us. We must turn this situation around. There's a Chinese saying: "When one becomes so accustomed to danger that it feels normal, the soul is lost."

We need to become "energy cops" and police our intuitive environments, as well as grant our kids the right to do so, too. We must claim a calm and loving atmosphere for ourselves, at least in our own homes. We must insist on this place of spiritual renewal—not as a luxury—but as a foundation of intuitive health and well-being.

We owe this to our children and to ourselves.

Establishing More New Habits

— **Freshen the air.** One of the most frightening things kids can experience is the tension and anxiety that comes with an argument between their parents. It makes them feel scared and insecure. However, since people in relationships inevitably have conflicts at times, it's not possible (or even necessarily desirable) to avoid all collisions of opinion.

If disagreements are polluting your home, open the windows and doors and allow fresh air and energy to come in for a moment or two. Then light a dried-sage smudge stick (available in metaphysical bookstores) and let the sweet smoke fill the rooms. Ask all the feuding parties to go for a walk around the block until they cool off.

— **Bless your house.** Have each family member light a candle and then walk together from room to room, blessing your home. As you enter the living room, ask that it bring you pleasant company and positive memories; and when you get to the kitchen, pray that it nurtures your bodies and souls. In the bedrooms, request that they soothe and heal you as you sleep and send you sweet dreams.

If you're uncomfortable doing this, then simply have your family thank God in your own way for providing you all with a safe haven and sanctuary. Ask for continued protection and blessings.

— **Beautify your surroundings.** The human spirit thrives on harmony, beauty, and balance. To create these qualities in your home, you can paint the walls in calming colors, bring in fresh flowers, arrange your furniture in pleasant configurations, eliminate clutter and disorder, and burn incense. If your home is naturally dark, you can hang beautiful pictures and mirrors, use full-spectrum lightbulbs, and open the blinds and shades to let the sunshine in. Enhancing the light is important because it keeps energy moving. Love yourself and your family enough to care and make every room harmonious.

— **Dance and sing.** When you engage in the pleasure of music and movement, Spirit enters your body. A home that's alive with song and dance is also filled with grace, so put on your favorite album and let your feet take over.

— **Lower the volume.** Loud and dissonant noises disturb the spirit. Therefore, practice keeping the volume of the house at a pleasant level, including the sounds of televisions, stereos, and voices. Be conscious of how delicate we all are and the fact that we need a certain amount of calm to turn inward.

Reflections

- How would you describe the tone and energy of your home?

- Is it clutter free and organized? If not, how does this make you and your family members feel?

- What do you need to clean and clear out?

- Can you designate areas in your house for play and for calm? Where?

- Have you created a personal altar? If you have, how is it affecting you? Have you shared this idea with your children? How have they responded?

- Have you experimented with aromatherapy? If so, have you noticed how it affects you and the other members of your family?

- Have you tried playing some form of classical music in your home? What kind?

- Have you noticed an increase in awareness and sensitivity in your kids since you've begun to consciously raise the energy level?

- Do you have plants, animals, or fish? Are there living things in each room? Can you sense how their vibrations influence the atmosphere?

- Is your own vibration clear? Are you free of emotional clutter? The personal energy you emanate into your environment is the most influential of all. Is yours calming and vitalizing, or are you toxic, angry, and tense? If you're sending out negativity, what are your plans for changing this in order to heal?

Reminders

Are you:

- Meditating daily?
- Simplifying your schedule?
- Tuning in to your heart?
- Keeping your house clutter free and serene?

Now that you have a deeper understanding of how the body responds to energy and have some new tools for creating a more healing atmosphere in your home, we'll look at how you can become more aware of your personal vibration as well as your children's.

PART II

Accepting the Gift

In this section, we'll focus on how you can begin to accept intuition as a gift from Spirit and welcome it into your home. You'll do this in several ways:

1. You'll learn creative approaches to acknowledging and expressing the six-sensory feelings that are part of your spiritual anatomy.

2. You'll get a deeper understanding of how energy affects us all, and will explore various tools for establishing better personal boundaries and psychic protection for yourself and your children.

3. Finally, you'll discover some of the common blind spots and bad habits that interrupt the unfolding of your kids' intuition as well as your own. You'll be given some techniques that will help you overcome these unconscious tendencies.

Hopefully, by the end of Part II, you will have made the transition from awakening your own sixth sense to sparking your children's intuition, and will be well on your way toward receiving the gifts of Spirit in your home.

Chapter Five

AWAKENING TO THE
WORLD OF VIBRATION

The most significant difference between how I grew up and the experience of some of my friends was that in my family, we were taught that there are no boundaries between the material, emotional, and intuitive realms. We learned that everything exists on one plane of energy.

Being an avid student of metaphysics, my mom instructed us in a concept that quantum physicists now corroborate: Everything on our planet—every table, chair, plant, and child—is composed of energy in motion. Although objects and people look different from each other because of their varying vibratory rates, they're all made of the same essential matter. In our household, this idea translated as an ability to recognize that thoughts and emotions are as solid and distinct as the floor under our feet. My mother would often say to us, "I can feel what's going through your mind, so you'd better think straight."

We never believed that simply because something was out of sight, it was out of mind. In fact, we often picked up vibes at a distance, such as having a feeling that Dad was getting ice cream to surprise us, and arriving home to find that he had. Or we'd sense that Aunt Emma was going to phone to ask us to visit for the night, only to have her call an hour or so later to invite us. Frequently, my mom would announce that so-and-so must be thinking about her because that person had popped into her mind. It wasn't at all unusual for her to interrupt us in midsentence, holding one finger up to her lips to hush us while she turned inward. "Sh!" she'd say, as though listening to some intuitive broadcast. And we'd all sit in silence as she tuned in to another frequency.

This ability to connect to one another on the six-sensory level became a family trademark. It was as though we each had our own personal music or song that we'd send out on a telepathic wavelength. We all soon became very familiar with everyone's unique vibrations and could recognize them immediately, like a well-known song.

What's a Personal Vibration?

My studies have taught me that one's personal vibration is the combined energy of the physical body, the emotional state, and the etheric or intuitive consciousness. When this synthesis is in harmony, it creates a grounded, peaceful frequency that's like a well-composed piece of music. However, if any one of the elements of the self is out of balance, the vibes become dissonant or off-key. Someone who's sensitive can tell when another person is disturbed, usually feeling it in their heart, chest, or stomach area. Such awareness can alert perceptive parents to a problem and guide them to take steps to help their children regain their inner equilibrium.

I recall sitting in the kitchen one day after school with a few girlfriends, my two sisters, and my mother, just laughing and talking about the day. All of a sudden, my mom shushed us, "Be quiet! Something's going on."

We all shut up instantly, trying to focus on what she was picking up. Abruptly, she asked, "Where's Anthony?" None of us knew where my brother was, so she continued to concentrate. "He's been hurt . . . I can feel it!"

Tense, we sat silently, wondering what exactly could be going on. No more than ten minutes had passed when the phone rang. It was the Denver Health Medical Center. Apparently, Anthony had been in an accident coming home from school. The car he was riding in had been struck from behind, and he'd gone right through the windshield. My mother had tuned in to his physical energy at the moment of the impact, and it was as though she'd been hit, too. Luckily, he'd only suffered a few cuts and bruises. He was stitched up and released from the hospital two hours later.

The incident left a huge impression on me. It taught me just how far our vibrations can travel and how much they can be felt. We are indeed far more than our bodies.

A few years later, I had another experience with my mom's telepathic abilities. We kids were entering our teen years and were going to rock concerts, dating, and generally spreading our wings. One winter evening, my brother Neil set off with his friends for a concert in Steamboat Springs. It was a very cold, snowy night; and they traveled 60 miles into the mountains to get there. At 1 in the morning, the phone rang and woke my parents. It was the police, who informed my father that Neil had been in a car wreck and was seriously injured. They said that he'd been taken by ambulance to a local hospital and that his chances for survival didn't look good.

My dad was terribly upset and told my mom what had happened. At first she was frantic, but then a calm came over her.

"It's not him," she stated.

"What?!" he responded in disbelief. "They have his driver's license, and he's been taken to the emergency room. Now hurry up and let's go!"

"No, it isn't him. I can feel his vibration, and he's perfectly well."

My father ignored her and quickly got dressed, but my mother just sat there motionless. Ten minutes later, just as my father was about to leave, the phone rang again. It was Neil, who was very agitated.

"Dad, I'm at the hospital," he said.

"Are you all right?" my father asked.

"I'm fine, but there was an accident in front of us on the way home. The driver lost control, swerved into the other lane, and collided with an oncoming car. We stopped and helped the people until the police came."

"But they just called and told us that *you* were the one hurt. They found your driver's license in your coat pocket."

"No, it wasn't me . . . I put my jacket over the guy who *was* injured, and my wallet was in it," Neil explained. "Don't worry, it was just a mistake."

My father hung up, feeling greatly relieved and a little shocked about the whole bizarre incident. He turned to my mom and said, "That was Neil. Evidently, he's okay."

She smiled and started to cry, "I *told* you it wasn't his vibration."

We All Have a Personal Vibration

We all have a personal vibration that's as unique as our finger-prints or the sound of our voice. Our energy pattern relays every-thing about us—physically, emotionally, and intuitively. It indicates if we're strong or weak, happy or sad, sick or healthy, grounded or unmoored, and focused or lost. It even shows whether we're aware or unconscious.

Becoming conscious of your own vibration means teaching yourself to notice and respond to the subtle energies of your being. This awareness originates in the heart; and it takes sensitivity, effort, and attention if you're to succeed in developing it. However, as I tell my students, it's no different from learning to appreciate music, which to the uneducated ear is only a pleasant blur of sound. But as you increase your focus, you can heighten your perceptions and begin to discern the individual instruments that blend together to create such beauty.

The first step is shifting your attention away from your head and the world of thoughts and words, and slipping instead into your heart and the realm of feeling tones. It's not about making an intellectual connection but an intuitive one. Do you remember when you fell in love? Do you recall times when the phone rang and you *knew* it was (or wasn't) your beloved? What you were tap-ping into was a personal vibration. It's like your calling card—as exclusively yours as your personality.

Children—and especially infants—are naturally good at recog-nizing vibes. It's how they know when you're planning to leave the house before you've even made the final decision to do so. It's also why they run to the door in anticipation of greeting you before you get home; quietly cower in the corner when they sense that you're angry, sad, or fearful; and draw near you, wanting to share your energy when they feel you're happy.

You can recover the innate ability to tune in to vibrations, including your family members'. Check in with your heart and ask yourself if everything seems to be well with them. Look at each person one by one through the awareness of your heart, and listen with complete compassion. Observe their movements, tone, and vibes. Remember that this is very subtle, and avoid letting your expectation that you'll detect strong feelings negate what you actually do experience. With practice, you'll be able to pick up more and more, especially if you're grounded in your own energy and are clearheaded.

You can further tune in to someone's personal vibration by consciously noticing all that you can when you're with them—in other words, by paying attention to what's emanating *from* them, whether it's calm, quiet, agitated, frightened, healthy, sick, strong, or weak. You can feel your children's energy patterns by rocking them, massaging their backs, holding their hands, and listening to their voices and heartbeats. All of the activities that we often call "bonding" are really about becoming familiar with another person's vibes.

Sour Notes

Because a personal vibration is composed of physical, emotional, and intuitive energy, it can be weakened by any number of things, including health problems, stress, exhaustion, or poor nutrition. Too much sugar, alcohol, or drugs; being upset, angry, or afraid; and negative people who drain or frighten us are also all detrimental.

Just as a sensitive musician can identify a "sour note," parents who are aware and connected to their hearts will notice when a child's vibes are off-key. It usually begins as a very subtle shift, and many times moms and dads will choose to ignore it, wanting more concrete proof that something is wrong. However, if we'd stop doubting our wisdom, and instead trust our intuition about our kids, many problems could be corrected before they got out of hand.

My client Allen is the divorced father of a boy and a girl. One day his son, Larry, visited him and seemed fine, but as Allen later told me, "He seemed off by one shade, and it bothered me." He called his ex-wife and quizzed her: Was Larry okay? Did he seem all right to her?

She assured him that he was perfectly well, but Dad wasn't satisfied. He asked Larry many questions about his life, health, and state of mind; and with some prodding, got the boy to admit that he didn't feel great and had been pretty tired lately. He'd just been covering it up because he didn't want to create more problems between his parents.

Although Allen's ex-wife thought he was being obsessive, he followed his heart and insisted that Larry get a checkup. The next day he took his son to the doctor, who found that the child's blood count was abnormal and diagnosed leukemia. Fortunately, thanks to his very alert and intuitive father, he was treated early and is now in remission. Allen often wonders what would have happened if he hadn't noticed and trusted his feelings and pushed the issue.

Another client, Dylan, also knew her seven-year-old son John's vibration well enough to sense that something wasn't right with him when he started second grade. He was an extremely bright kid who was even considered gifted by his teachers, so Dylan had no reason to worry about him, but in her heart she did. When she voiced her feelings to her husband, he said he thought she was being a worry-wart, but even his criticism and dismissal didn't deter her.

Finally, acting purely on her instinct, she had John tested at a learning center. There they discovered that he had severe dyslexia and gradual hearing loss. The reason why this hadn't been apparent was that he had a photographic memory that allowed him to compensate for his difficulties. They immediately set about getting him educational assistance and support, and in less than two years, John was also wearing a hearing aid. Because Dylan had been truly aware of her son's vibration and trusted her gut feeling that he needed to be checked, his problems were diagnosed early enough to avoid more serious setbacks.

You can protect and help your children, too, if you become attuned to their personal energy patterns. Whether they're experiencing physical or intuitive distress, kids send you signals when they're out of balance that you need to notice.

Trust Your Heart

Living a six-sensory life is about being as comfortable with your nonphysical dimensions as your physical ones. It means being able to sense and acknowledge vibrations as readily as you notice stoplights and street signs. When you're aware of your children's personal vibrations, you'll be alerted whenever anything is off on any level, but the knowledge alone won't bring everything back into balance. It's only when you trust your heart, respond to its signals, and *act* on your instincts that your intuition will begin to serve you and your family well. Know that you *can* sense their invisible energy fields, and simply honor your feelings without question.

Your kids take their cues from you. Therefore, if you freely acknowledge your subtle, heart-based inclinations and say so, they will, too. It's incredibly refreshing when that happens! It's calling a spade a spade.

Several years ago, I was working at home on a writing project and was feeling terribly pressured. My anxiety spilled over into the atmosphere, and soon I could feel my daughter Sabrina reacting to the tension. I was sitting at one end of the room writing, while she was working on a project of her own at the other end. We were both silent and deep in concentration, but after 15 minutes, she stood up.

"That's it, Mom! I have to go downstairs. You're filling up all the space with bad feelings, and I can't breathe. I need oxygen!" And she collected her stuff and walked out. On her way out the door, she yelled back at me, "You shouldn't work so hard. Your energy is *off!*"

Her point was well taken. I put down my pen, took a deep breath, and began to laugh. Then I got up and went for a bike ride. My personal vibration obviously needed a tune-up!

It doesn't matter whose energy is out of balance or who feels it first. Pay attention to your family and get to know their individual vibes. One child may have a solid, grounded feeling; and another may be more ethereal. A person who's athletic may be more robust than one who's sensitive and artistic, but this doesn't mean that kids can't be both strong *and* imaginative, because some are. Everyone is unique, and it's up to you to become familiar with your child's energetic personality—your sixth sense will guide you.

When you know your children's vibes, you'll sense when they're off-kilter. Always take these instincts seriously and act on them as they arise. Don't wait for someone else to give you permission to feel your own feelings. Set an example for your kids by trusting yourself.

Whether it's a matter of physical well-being, artistic disposition, social requirements, or spiritual integrity, act on your own intuition as if it were the most important thing in the world. In fact, it is!

What about Your Own Personal Vibration?

Everyone in your family has a distinct personal vibration, including you; and when yours is disrupted, your sensitivity and perception of your children and spouse will be compromised. Conditions such as excessive negativity, anger, extreme stress, sickness, and exhaustion, as well as addictions and a poor diet, can throw your intuition out of balance and interfere with your clarity and ability to tune in to your loved ones.

These influences can play tricks on your awareness, causing one of two consequences. The first is what I call hypersensitivity, which is when your intuition goes haywire and you begin picking up anything and everything that's in the "ethers," so to speak. This is the psychic equivalent of tuning in to ten radio stations at the same time; and can lead to confusion, overreaction, anxiety attacks, and outbursts, causing you to lose your clear, grounded consciousness of what's really going on.

The second effect that adverse conditions can cause is to completely tune out your six-sensory awareness. You may disconnect, develop tunnel vision, and see only what you want to. As a result, you miss the bigger picture, fail to understand what the situation really requires, and distance yourself from your kids.

The way to avoid both consequences is to be responsible about maintaining balance in your life, and develop practices that support good mental health. Relax, exercise, and meditate; don't overwork; and avoid or address any addictions. Get the facts instead of being run by your fears. Finally, stay optimistic and connected to your heart.

Establishing New Habits

— **Take mental breathers.** To keep your awareness grounded, and to ensure that the vibes you receive about your family and life remain clear and accurate, practice what I call "mental breathers." Take one or two daily breaks of about five to ten minutes each. Stop whatever you're doing and simply relax into a moment of tranquility. You might choose to savor a cup of tea (not coffee—too much caffeine!), enjoy a quick stroll around the block, or just sit back and look out the window. These time-outs will strengthen and tone your personal vibration and rebalance any minor dissonance you may be experiencing.

Establishing this habit will create an inner oasis you can retreat to whenever you're feeling agitated, annoyed, or worried. It will also keep your intuition sharp and steady. By taking regular breaks, you'll get better at differentiating between true "bad vibes" and simple static or imbalance within yourself.

— **Make a note of it.** One of the more exciting ways to learn to tune in to personal vibrations is to carry around a pocket notebook or tape recorder. Every time you feel any little hint, twinge, vibe, or subtle notion regarding a child or other family member, rather than mulling it over and wondering whether it's valid, simply notice what you're experiencing and write it down or record it. For example, you might note: "Anna was very nervous and subdued after school today. I wonder if something or someone upset her." Or, "I've been thinking about Phil all day. Is his trip to see his father going smoothly?" Describing your feelings accomplishes two important things: First, it tells your subconscious mind that you now intend to pay attention to and value your intuition. Second, it frees you from the temptation to ignore its messages.

My client Marianne tried this tool with her own kids. She told me that at first, she felt almost as though she were making up feelings just to have something to write about. But after just a week of practicing this technique, she got an overwhelming vibe that her 16-year-old daughter, Ida, who was on her first unchaperoned camping trip with two girlfriends, was in trouble. After Marianne noted her impression, it only became stronger—so strong, in fact, that she felt compelled to drive to the campsite where she knew they'd be. Feeling silly, she nevertheless decided to follow her hunch.

When she got there, she discovered her daughter and the other girls huddled around their car, attempting to fix a flat tire in the dark. As soon as Ida saw her mom pull up, she screamed for joy. The teenagers didn't have a clue about what they were doing, and what should have been a relatively simple task had turned into a frustrating predicament. Ida was particularly worried that they might be stranded; and even though the situation wasn't dire, they were all scared to be in such a bind in the middle of nowhere. They were thrilled to see Marianne arrive. "Mom, I kept sending you vibes to help us." Ida said. "I can't believe you actually got them!"'

Writing down or recording your perceptions clears your mind and sharpens your awareness. If you do it regularly, you'll receive feedback on the importance of what you're noticing in no time at all.

— **Speak up.** Share any personal vibrations you may have with your family and encourage them to do the same. This will demonstrate to your children that you regard the subtle, nonphysical realm of energy as highly as you do the physical plane.

In my home, we tune in to each other's vibes and openly express what we're picking up, as well as sharing our own feelings.

For example, when my daughter Sonia was in the second grade, I had a sense that something was off and asked her if anything was out of balance. At first she insisted that she was fine, but after a few minutes, she reconsidered. "I'm not really okay," she said. "I'm having trouble with French, and I feel like the other kids in my class think I'm dumb." Then she burst into tears. Once my feeling was confirmed, Patrick and I began to give her a lot more support, and she found her confidence once again in no time.

Sharing personal vibes helps us connect to our hearts; clears the air; and makes everyone's awareness crisp, keen, and sharp—the perfect conditions for activating intuition. After doing this exercise for a while, we've fine-tuned our sensitivity to one another to a very caring and gentle level. It keeps us conscious of how vulnerable we all are and prevents us from falling into ruts of disregarding each other. It also keeps our perception clear and opens us to inspiration.

False Alarms vs. Real Problems

Inevitably, the highest priority for parents is the safety of their children. Fortunately, having a true familiarity with your kids' personal vibrations will help you protect them.

"But how do I know if I'm tuning in to real problems or just getting worked up over nothing?" one eager but anxious mother asked me. "I often worry a lot about my son, especially when he's traveling by plane. If I'm not careful, I can go into a full-blown panic attack until he's arrived safely. Is that an accurate vibe or a false alarm?"

This is a good question, and probably the most important one for moms and dads. If you also frequently agonize about the well-being of your children (and nearly *all* parents do at one time or another), it's important to know that the source of the distress you're feeling *is* psychic in nature, but it doesn't necessarily mean that disaster is pending.

What actually happens at these anxious times is that the intuitive bond you have with your child temporarily gets cut off, much as a radio loses a particular station signal for a little while when there's interference. This disconnection can happen because of worry, confusion, or sometimes even the youngster's own desire for freedom and independence, especially if you're an overly controlling or domineering parent. It's usually the psychic separation itself that alarms you rather than an outside threat or premonition. The fact that you can't feel the energy at all is what causes your uneasiness and the tendency to start imagining all kinds of worst-case scenarios. Most likely, your child is just fine. When you do experience such disruptions, instead of working yourself into a nervous wreck, you can use the following tool:

Renewing Connections

If you feel disconnected from your children (or a particular child), simply focus on your heart and think about them. Say their names to yourself and ask Divine Spirit to surround them with the pure white light of loving protection. Imagine that this brilliant halo completely envelops them and whoever else they might come into contact with, wherever they are. See them in your mind's eye as safe and in total peace. And while you're at it, send them your love.

This visualization will help you reconnect with their vibration and guard them from all dangers anywhere in the world. You'll be doing something to balance both your own energy pattern and your kids', as well as reestablishing the connection you share.

Right vs. Wrong

As you begin to tune in to the world of energy, there will be times when you may experience what appear to be the false alarms that we just discussed. For example, you may have a worrisome feeling about your child, yet it turns out that everything is just fine. Does that mean that your intuition isn't reliable?

Not necessarily. When it comes to the sixth sense, being "right" shouldn't be your absolute goal, especially when you're just beginning to become more sensitive. It's a high-level skill that requires you to practice a lot and make many errors if you're to become good at it. And besides, you might actually be tuning in to a precarious situation where real danger or imbalance does indeed exist, but the issue may somehow right itself before it becomes a serious problem. After all, energy isn't fixed, but is always in a state of motion.

My client Janice, a very intuitive and aware mother, told me about her experience with her 17-year-old daughter, Lisa. Janice offered to chaperone Lisa and her girlfriends on a spring-break trip to Cancún. Wanting to give her daughter space while still being there to supervise, Janice stayed in a separate room during the five days of their vacation.

One morning, Lisa told her mom that she and her friends were going to the beach, and they agreed to meet at 5 o'clock for dinner. All day long, Janice had a terrible feeling about her daughter's vibration and worried that she wasn't okay. Her emotions fluctuated from mild worry to moments of real psychic upset. *What's going on with her?* she asked herself, certain something was off. Finally, she calmed down and surrounded Lisa with white light, and gradually the anxiety faded.

At last the dinner hour rolled around, and Janice called her daughter's room. "She's in the shower," said Chris, one of the roommates. "Hold on, I'll see if she's out yet."

While she was waiting, Janice could hear the girls talking, including Chris exclaiming, "Thank God I stopped Lisa from having sex on the beach today!"

Janice almost dropped the receiver. *No wonder I was so upset!* she thought. *What was Lisa thinking? What were they up to?*

A moment later, Lisa picked up the phone. "Hi, Mom!" she said, sounding like her usual cheerful self.

"I need to talk to you!" replied Janice, trying to contain her righteous indignation and alarm. "Please come to my room right now."

Lisa strolled in a few minutes later and sat down. Unable to restrain herself any longer, Janice blurted out, "I overheard Chris say that she stopped you from having sex on the beach! What on earth were you doing?"

Lisa was surprised and puzzled. "I don't know what you're talking about, Mom. We were together the whole time."

"I had terrible vibes about you all afternoon, and there's no point in trying to cover up. I could feel that you were up to something!"

Lisa seemed confused for a moment, and then burst out laughing. "I'm sorry, Mom! I just figured it out! 'Sex on the Beach' is the name of one of the vodka drinks they were selling at the bar, and I was thinking of trying one."

Greatly relieved, even Janice had to chuckle.

Were her vibes off? I don't think so. After all, a 17-year-old girl shouldn't be drinking alcohol, much less in a foreign country! Did her mother's prayers and visualizations help? Well, Lisa never did have "Sex on the Beach"!

Recognizing vibrations isn't about "right" or "wrong," but about tuning in to energy in motion and keeping it balanced. It isn't static—it's fluid and alive and changes with the circumstances. Lisa was temporarily in a position to hurt herself, which her mom accurately sensed. Perhaps it was Janice's prayer that turned the situation around and restored equilibrium. I believe it was.

Recognizing your children's personal vibrations—and especially any energy imbalances or threats—is an ability that's centered in the heart. It requires awareness, sensitivity, and groundedness; but with practice, it can become as natural as breathing. Enjoying mental breaks, practicing meditation, keeping yourself in physical and emotional balance, maintaining a healing home environment, and taking the time to bond with your kids are the essential keys to keeping your intuitive lifeline to them strong and intact.

Establishing More New Habits

— **Exchange energy.** While breathing gently, put one hand on your own heart and the other on your child's. With your eyes closed, sense his or her energy and ask your heart to show you if there's any dissonance, whether physical, emotional, or mental. Don't be overly analytical—simply relax and accept whatever comes up. Then open your eyes and share your feelings if the child is old enough to understand. If not, write down your observations in a notebook.

You can do this exercise from a distance, by *visualizing* placing your hand on your child's heart. You might also want to teach your kids how to do this—it's a technique they love to practice, and they can use it their entire lives.

— **Get up close and personal.** When you're with your children, shut your eyes for a moment and, with full awareness, notice the physical sensations you have when you're close to them, hug them, and hear and feel them breathing. Inhale as you do this, and then do the same exercise with your eyes open.

— **Hand it over.** Give your child a hand or foot massage for five minutes. Don't talk as you do so, but simply focus your awareness on her body, noticing how your energy affects her—and remember to breathe! As you work, observe whether she seems calm or restless, vibrant or weak. Is she open to receiving energy, or is she blocking your attention? Do you notice anything else? When you're finished, ask her how she felt during the experience. Then reverse your roles and have her give *you* a short massage.

— **Stabilize and heal personal vibrations.** Begin by closing your eyes and quieting your vibes with a few deep, relaxing breaths. Next, focus your full attention on the center of your heart and acknowledge three things that you love about yourself. Be fair, generous, and gentle; and feel the flow of compassion and self-acceptance moving throughout your entire energy field. Now tenderly say your child's name and visualize placing him in the center of your heart.

Send the same flow of care and acceptance to him, imagining that it begins deep within his own heart and streams outward, filling up his entire being. See him completely engulfed in your love—you're appreciating, healing, calming, and balancing his vibration. Do this for two or three minutes, and when you're finished, open your eyes.

— **Send love**. There are many opportunities to connect with your child throughout the day. Send love by:

- Looking into your child's eyes for two minutes without speaking.

- Waking her *gently* in the morning.

- Tucking her into bed with a leisurely "Good night."

- Looking into her eyes and saying, "I love you."

- Observing how she moves, speaks, sits, talks, and plays, paying attention to any subtle shifts and asking your heart to help you notice when anything is off balance.

- Putting a white loving light of protection around your child every day (and surrounding yourself with this light, too).

Reflections

- Practice paying attention to each family member's unique vibration. Can you describe your partner's, your child's, and your own?

- Are you able to identify when a loved one's vibes are off-kilter? When yours are? Do you acknowledge this?

- Do you have any special "bonding" activities that you do with your spouse and children that help you connect with their personal energy patterns?

- Are you aware of your own vibes? If not, are you taking care of your mental, physical, and emotional health and well-being so that you'll develop your ability to tune in to them?

- As you become more conscious of personal vibrations, are you noticing more about your kids? Your mate? Yourself?

- Have you had any intuitive insights regarding your loved ones or yourself? If so, what are they?

Reminders

Are you:

- Tuning in to your heart?
- Simplifying your schedule?
- Keeping your house clutter free and serene?
- Noticing subtle vibrations and picking up energy patterns?

Special Note

Another way to bring your personal vibration back into balance is with flower essences, which are liquid extracts derived from various plants and blossoms through distillation. The most famous are the Bach Flower Remedies, a collection of 38 different extracts that are specifically designed to heal emotional or intuitive dissonance and restore harmony. Flower essences and information about their benefits can be found in most health-food stores or online. Keep in mind that although these products can help you recover your psychic and emotional equilibrium, they can't take the place of basic health care, good food, and an emotionally sound atmosphere.

Nonetheless, they're wonderful supplements and can bring about great shifts in your personal vibration. Check them out for yourself!

✳ ✳ ✳

Chapter Six

THE LANGUAGE OF SPIRIT

One of my psychic mentors, Charlie Goodman, taught me something very important about awakening intuition. He said that the difference between having a feeling and actually *expressing* it makes all the difference in the world.

"Being aware of intuition is only one part of the process," he'd tell me. "Communicating it is the other. When you do so, you're putting value on your sixth sense, and then it can begin to help you in life."

Because so many people didn't grow up in families where intuition was acknowledged, they often feel awkward or uncomfortable about openly expressing their inner awareness. To a large degree, this may be simply due to the fact that they don't have a language that allows them to share their insights easily and without self-consciousness.

When some individuals do talk about their feelings, they call them "weird," "funny," "bizarre," "creepy," or "scary." The problem with these terms is that their connotations are negative, and intuition becomes associated with something unpleasant. If you say you had a "weird experience," for example, many people will automatically look at you as if *you* are abnormal—no matter what actually happened to you. And as most parents know, no child wants to be thought of as a freak! Kids are very sensitive about how they're perceived by their peers, and being seen as "different" causes them to suffer. They'd rather ignore their inner voice instead . . . and they do.

Another more cavalier way in which people describe their intuitive experiences is as "odd incidents" or "strange coincidences." This vocabulary allows them to both acknowledge six-sensory events and dismiss them as flukes, aberrations, and certainly nothing of significance.

Probably the best expressions for vibes are the "organic" ones that show where the energy is being picked up in the body, such as "a gut feeling," "a tight chest," "a lump in my throat," or " butterflies in my stomach." But these common phrases often aren't taken seriously.

In my family, intuition was so fundamental to our way of life that we actually had specific "code words" to acknowledge and express our higher wisdom. These terms were quite simple yet conveyed extremely complex feelings. This language made it easy for us to share what we felt, bypassing the intellectual and emotional barriers that explanations create. The very fact that we had special words for our various six-sensory flashes taught us that our inner perceptions were valid and worth noticing.

The first of our code words is *vibes,* which means the initial energetic sensation of intuition in the body. We divided vibes into categories: *Good vibes* are the happy, positive feelings evoked when we encounter people, places, ideas, synchronicities, and possibilities that are beneficial to us. Getting good vibes gives us a sense of protection and grace, and indicates a "green light" or that we should "go for it" when we have a decision to make.

We also had *bad vibes,* which refers to all the uncomfortable feelings that caution us: "Keep away," "Don't do it," "Don't trust it," "Watch out," "Be careful," or "Stay on your toes!" They're instincts that alert us that something isn't okay.

In addition, we had words that described other intuitive states. *Grounded,* for example, means the sensation of being present, solid, secure, strong, and committed. In contrast, *ungrounded* is the state of being rushed, overwhelmed, overloaded, disconnected, out of harmony with our surroundings, uncomfortable, ill at ease, nervous, defensive, irritable, and vulnerable.

You can see how many subtle states these few words encompass, and you can doubtless understand what a relief it was to us children to be able to express so much, so simply. We gave no more thought to having bad vibes than to seeing a red car—they were merely another part of our sensory landscape. Growing up with such a basic vocabulary to communicate intuition has made it extremely easy for me to integrate my sixth sense into my adult life as just another everyday aspect of my awareness.

I've continued the tradition of "speaking the language of intuition" with my husband and our daughters. I've introduced them to the terms that are so familiar to me, and together we've invented others. Sonia came up with *woolies* to describe how she feels when someone or something disrupts her inner harmony. It also refers to the conditions or people who irritate her—like wool on bare skin. When she says someone "gives her the woolies," I understand that she feels uncomfortable around them. This was good to know when she was younger and was invited to many of her classmates' birthday parties. If a "wooly" asked her to come, she simply begged off, sure she wouldn't like it. It kept her from enduring an unpleasant experience or having to explain to us *why* she didn't want to go. The fact that she felt someone was a wooly was explanation enough.

Another term we use in our home is *wide open*. This means that we're taking in more stimulation than feels comfortable, and it's causing us to become ungrounded. As an adult, you may experience being wide open when you're unexpectedly called in to the boss's office, only to be criticized—or worse yet, let go. It can happen when you pick up the phone and someone "lets you have it." You know the feeling: It's being overwhelmed, caught off guard, and taken by surprise.

My family also refers to "shutting down," which is a way of protecting yourself from unwanted influences. There are two ways to do this: One is to imagine that you're closing yourself off to negativity, just as you'd shut a window or door to prevent unpleasant elements from coming at you from outside. The second option is to walk away from a harmful situation to escape its effects. Of course, you can always use both methods at the same time to keep yourself safe from undesirable energy.

I was with Sonia at the airport one day, waiting to check in luggage, when the man in front of us threw a fit at the counter. He was causing such a scene over his reservation mix-up that he'd managed to get three ticket agents involved, and now they were beginning to argue among themselves. Their agitation was spilling over to the crowd of waiting passengers, who were beginning to yell at him to "Shut up" and "Move on." It was an ugly situation and was getting worse.

Without a second thought, Sonia turned to me and said, "Uh-oh . . . trouble. Better shut down and ignore it." And she was right. Otherwise, like the other people around us, we would have absorbed the tension.

Respond When Intuition Speaks

Using simple expressions such as the ones I discussed above sends a huge message to children about the importance of their intuition. It says, "I understand," "I believe you," "I feel it, too," "I recognize this energy as real," and—last but not least—"Let's take action to protect ourselves and respond to this information."

For example, several years ago on the Fourth of July, all the families on our block closed off the street to have a party and neighborhood picnic, which is an annual tradition. The kids ran around, rode bikes, and played games all day long; and in the evening, we shared a potluck dinner. At dusk, a few parents brought out fireworks, and adults and children alike sat down to watch.

After about 30 minutes of blasts and kabooms, Sabrina approached me and whispered, "Mom, for some reason I'm scared. There's too much excitement for me. I feel uncomfortable and have bad vibes. I'm too wide open, and I don't like it."

Sonia, on the other hand, was loving it and wanted to carry on. By nature, she's a lot more grounded than Sabrina, and the wild energy wasn't affecting her as much. When I checked with her about her vibes, she said that she sensed some agitation, too, but not enough to want to leave the show.

Sabrina wanted to go home, which was fine with me. She needed to say no more. We went inside, but not before I told Patrick, who'd been standing some distance away, how the girls felt. Just to play it safe, he decided to move all the kids another 15 feet away from the fireworks, and to keep Sonia close to him.

Moments later, from inside the house, Sabrina and I heard a flurry of explosions and screams. Seconds later, Sonia rushed in, out of breath. "You should have seen what just happened!" she exclaimed.

Patrick came in behind her, looking shaken. "Those bad vibes you had were right on target, Sabrina! When Joe set off the Turbo Man [the grand finale of the fireworks], it tipped onto its side and fired straight into the crowd! No one was hurt, but it was too close for comfort. We just averted a disaster and decided that was enough for one night."

Sabrina replied, "I'm glad I wasn't there . . . my vibes told me to leave."

We all went to bed that night feeling very relieved.

As this story illustrates, having code words like *vibes, grounded, wide open,* or *shut down* gives kids a great way to express what their intuition is telling them without having to justify their feelings.

Simple Words, Protective Measures

Another family expression that my kids appreciate is _ick attack_. Its meaning is instantly clear—it's the icky or disgusted feeling you get when you're around someone or something with highly unpleasant energy.

I remember when I was in the ninth grade and going to Catholic school, I got a major *ick* attack every time I was around the girls' volleyball coach. All the young ladies loved him, and he seemed nice enough on the surface; but every time I was around him, he made me feel icky and invaded in some way, so I tried to avoid him outside class at all costs.

When my friend Gina confessed to me in the tenth grade that she'd been having sex with him for more than a year, I was revolted but not surprised. No wonder he'd given me such bad vibes! He was nothing more than a pervert—a slimy, *icky* one.

An additional code term I've been introduced to and have shared with my children is *psychic attack,* which is any mean-spirited, negative behavior that's intended to hurt you. Stronger than an *ick* attack, a warning against something or someone who's unpleasant or unhealthy, a psychic attack is when someone or something is actually trying to hurt you. This occurs all the time. It's the ambush from the co-worker who wants your job, the flaky friend who blames you for his mistake, the malicious neighbor who competes with you, or the alcoholic in a rage. This term describes mean-spirited, negative behavior that's directed toward you. It's very hurtful, and it's extremely important to arm your children with the ability to recognize the attack for what it is and move away from it when it occurs.

Psychic attacks feel like assaults, wounds, or injuries. However, they're harmful not only because they're painful, but because they cause you to doubt yourself. The very real arrows of venomous thoughts thrown your way can have lasting consequences.

It may not be obvious, but kids face this situation frequently—especially teenagers, with their insecurity and lack of power. When they're attacked, they feel hurt and may not know what hit them. But something *has* happened: a damaging vibration has burned right into their energy field.

Many children experience these intuitive injuries and don't know what to do. It causes them to shut down, withdraw, and feel insecure. It's therefore extremely important, as I mentioned, to arm them with the ability to recognize when they're being bombarded and move out of harm's way instead of reacting like so many people (particularly kids) do—by internalizing the negativity, which then becomes shame. They need to be taught to understand what's happening and talk to you about it. In the next chapter, I'll discuss what you can do to help your children restore their balance when they suffer a psychic attack. Right now, you can begin giving them the vocabulary to describe their experiences.

Your Words Are the Right Ones

Because of my work as a professional intuitive, my children have learned from the very beginning about the extremely subtle levels of psychic energy and ways to discuss them. It's not at all unusual for me to talk with them not only about vibes, *ick* attacks, and so forth, but also about energy fields, auras, chakras, and other highly sophisticated concepts. Although this vocabulary works well for my family, it's *not* at all essential to use our particular lexicon in order to tap into the wonderful voice of inner awareness. You may prefer to refer to your intuition with more religious terms, such as *my angel* or even just *spirit*. Or you might like easy and obvious phrases, including *my gut, my hunch,* or *my feeling.* One family I know calls a psychic attack a "stink bomb," while another describes an *ick* attack as a "yucky feeling." Yet another has chosen to name their vibes their "radar." The point is that you can invent your own language of spirit. Whatever words *feel* right to you *are* the best ones for you.

Giving your kids a way to identify and talk about their six-sensory insights will help them integrate these experiences more comfortably into their lives. It's just so much easier for children to pay attention and respond to intuition if they don't have to *explain* what they feel—or worse, *why.* If they can just experience it, report it, and know that it will be respected, they'll be willing to share their inner guidance.

Know When to Keep a Secret

While psychic and intuitive feelings are natural, some people have a long way to go toward developing a balanced understanding of our six-sensory nature. Although the world is changing, misperceptions still abound, and they can and do shut down children's spontaneous expressions of their inner feelings.

My mother, who was savvy about the potential negative reactions her kids might face from unenlightened individuals, advised us to keep our code language a secret from disbelieving ears. She explained that people are either open-minded about the subject or they aren't, and that it's a waste of energy to talk about such things with those who aren't receptive.

"It's like speaking Greek to somebody who doesn't understand it. Why waste the time? Better to save it for those who do," she'd tell us.

It was good advice that spared me from the disparaging remarks of those who weren't "tuned in." I've shared the same wisdom with my own kids, and perhaps you may also want to suggest to your children that they keep their expressions for intuitive experiences a secret from those who might be inclined to make fun of them or give them a hard time about being six-sensory. Clue them in to the fact that some people, such as a skeptical and insensitive teacher, or (more likely) another child who hasn't been introduced to the world of psychic energy, may not be as receptive to vibes as they'd hope.

Body Language: The Most Direct Communication

In addition to code words, my family has another way to communicate that allows my daughters to convey their vibes freely and without fear—body language. We've agreed that in any situation, any one of us may take another's hand and share what we're feeling using a system of squeezes. For example, if Sonia or Sabrina is nervous, one squeeze of the hand means "I'm ungrounded; protect me." Two squeezes says "Bad vibes; I don't like it. Let's go!" And one long squeeze signals "Good vibes—I *do* like it." Our silent connection allows us to touch base with one another and our feelings in an even more profound way than words will allow.

If you have boys who don't like to hold hands, a few shoulder squeezes or arm taps can work in the same way. As a family, you can invent your own code, whether you use verbal or body language (or both). The important thing is to set up a system to communicate your insights freely and *privately*.

Developing a language of spirit creates a framework that helps your children express their inner voices without fear of censorship, as well as receive the benefits they bring. It also allows you and your kids to avoid the tendency (born of bad habits) to dismiss the sixth sense as invalid or unavailable. Instead, you'll give it the value it deserves.

Vibes are a natural part of who we are, and having a creative vocabulary that lets you easily describe them will support you in reclaiming intuition in your lives.

Establishing New Habits

— **Create your own private psychic code.** Ask your spouse and children to describe their intuition using their own special words. Together, have fun building a vocabulary that's all-encompassing and supports your inner guidance.

— **Discover what language they speak.** As a family, notice the descriptive words and phrases that other people use to communicate their intuition, and then talk about these expressions at home.

— **Be a secret agent.** Have your loved ones agree on several signals to share your six-sensory feelings with one another nonverbally. Ask each person for their input in creating a code that will protect and help everyone.

— **Write it down.** Jot down your household's favorite expressions for:

- An intuitive feeling
- A positive vibe
- A negative vibe

Also note your family's words for:

- Feeling energetically uncomfortable
- A psychic attack
- The woolies
- An *ick* attack
- Any other intuitive experiences you wish to describe

Reflections

- Did your family of origin have code words to express their intuition? What were they?

- Could you speak freely about your inner awareness as a child? Do you do so today?

- Do your kids talk openly about their vibes?

- Does your partner or spouse easily discuss his or her insights with you?

- Do your parents, siblings, and other relatives share their six-sensory feelings without hesitation? What expressions do they use?

- Do your loved ones use validating words to describe intuition? Or does the way they speak reveal discomfort, confusion, or dismissal of Divine wisdom?

- If you've introduced a language of spirit into your home, have you noticed any differences in your psychic awareness?

Reminders

Are you:

- Simplifying your schedule?
- Keeping your house clutter free and serene?
- Noticing subtle vibrations?
- Creating your own language of spirit?

Chapter Seven

BUILDING BOUNDARIES AND CREATING PERSONAL PROTECTION

As you continue to accept intuition as a natural part of your spiritual nature, you'll quickly burst into a whole new dimension of consciousness. You'll discover that awakening your inner knowing is like noticing stars. For the longest time, you can go along oblivious to the night sky. Then one evening you look up and see some sparkling stars. Taken by their lovely twinkle, your eyes are drawn into the blackness, seeking more. At first you may spot only a few . . . then more and still more become clear . . . until quite spontaneously your entire perception shifts, and suddenly the universe seems to explode with thousands upon thousands of brilliant lights. It's humbling to realize that although they were there all along, you're just now becoming aware of them for the first time.

As you begin to tune in to the realm of Spirit, your intuition will shine like the stars. Once you open to your higher guidance, you'll suddenly experience a surge of psychic perceptions, "Aha!" moments, and synchronous events, flowing like water. You and your family members will start to perceive others' energy fields; and the more you know about them, the better you'll be able to respond.

When my daughter Sonia was quite young, I was putting her to bed one night, and she asked, "Mom, did you know that people glow?"

"What do you mean?" I replied.

"I saw Bobby get really mad at Susan in school today, and when he was screaming at her, I saw a glowing red light just over his head—for real!" Sonia burst out laughing.

"You saw his aura, the energy field surrounding his body," I explained. "We all have one, and sometimes it can even absorb vibrations from others like a sponge. When someone gets angry, like Bobby did, their aura turns red. That's why people sometimes say, 'I was so furious that I saw red!' They really do."

I also told her that the energy field has many names, including "etheric body" (the word *etheric* stems from *ether,* which means "spirit"). It follows the outline of the physical self, extending from one to five feet beyond it.

A sensitive, intuitive person can sometimes perceive an aura, as Sonia did that morning. But even when we don't *see* it, it can still be felt; and it does affect us.

A Rainbow of Possibility

Our energy field can change in tone and color, depending upon how we feel—physically, mentally, and emotionally:

— When we're passionate, angry, or even frightened, our aura glows red and feels intense, brittle, and agitated. If we're tired or physically ill, it can become a muddy brown and we'll feel sticky, drained, and sluggish.

— When we're excited, delighted, inspired, or are experiencing pleasure, it turns bright orange and feels vibrant, energized, and alive.

— When we're deep in thought, concentrating, or trying to take control of things, it's a vivid yellow and feels intense, sharp, and dynamic.

— When we're feeling loved or loving or at peace with our surroundings, our energy field shines a brilliant green and is engaging, warm, and healing. When we experience kindness, affection, and romance, the green becomes speckled with pink tones and feels safe, calming, and compelling.

— When we're listening to our hearts or intuition or are in a state of receptivity—such as when we're learning or sharing ideas—our aura is sky blue and feels lucid, clear, and inspiring.

— If we have an active imagination or are visual thinkers, our etheric body radiates a deep indigo blue and feels adventurous, wise, and insightful.

— Finally, if we're in a state of prayer, meditation, or contemplation, or are feeling the love and guidance of the Universe, our energy field will become violet with flecks of gold, turning white around the edges. It will feel soothing, profound, and even sacred.

The changes in our aura's colors reflect our vitality, frame of mind, emotions, and physical condition. Since people—including children—are complex, their energy fields usually contain a blend of colors. When we're relaxed and conscious of the vibrations just beyond the material dimension, we can sense and sometimes see these auras.

Insight over Eyesight

The fact that Sonia was able to perceive Bobby's energy field was no big deal. I think all kids see auras at one time or another, usually when they're very young. Their eyes are attuned to these subtle frequencies because their minds are extremely clear and their hearts are open. They're so much more aware of their energetic surroundings than adults, who spend a great deal of time filtering out information because they're preoccupied with either past or future events.

Sue, a client of mine who'd adopted two children, made an appointment with me to discuss her four-year-old daughter Linda's unusual habit of talking about all the colors around each member of the family. "At times, she tells me she sees a yellow glow surrounding her brother's head," Sue said. "And once she mentioned that there was a pink light around my face. I know she's noticing our auras, Sonia, but I'm not exactly sure how to explain it to her."

Sue was right that Linda was tuning in to their auric fields, and I suggested that she simply tell her daughter the truth. "I think you may be surprised by how readily Linda will accept it," I encouraged her. "Just let her know that the energy she's observing surrounds everyone's bodies, and that she's lucky she can see it."

Sue followed my advice, and Linda responded, "So that's what that light is called. Okay." And that was the end of that.

I believe that as babies, we're all able to perceive auras. Some of us, like Linda, retain the ability for longer than others, but most lose it by the age of three or four. By then, our perspective has been sharply influenced, causing us to shift our focus *away* from the subtle energy planes to concentrate exclusively on the physical universe.

Resonance

Even if children stop seeing auras, they don't stop *feeling* or reacting to them, and with a little effort in awareness, neither do adults. Our auric fields are the sum total of our consciousness and personal vibration at any given time, and children can and do feel this consciousness quite acutely.

Whether we're feeling tense, angry, weak, tired, joyous, scared, or courageous, our aura reflects our emotional state. In addition, as we come into contact with other people's energy fields, we're affected by them and can even absorb their vibrations. This is good if we're around positive ones, but if we aren't careful, we can also be influenced by negativity.

Can you recall being around people so surly or unpleasant that you felt their energy crawling all over you like bugs, or draining you so much that you needed a nap? Remember how once you got away from them, you continued to feel their agitated vibes as though they were still next to you—sometimes so strongly that you became just as worked up as they were? This happened because their aura had contaminated your own.

Have you ever woken up on the wrong side of the bed and felt limp as a dishrag before you'd even shuffled to breakfast? Were you amazed that without saying a word, you caused the entire family to become edgy? In this case, your energy field infected the house.

On the other hand, have you spent time with a really caring, sweet person, such as a six-month-old baby in a good mood? Did you notice how their loving, open heart immediately lightened your own, leaving you feeling cheered and happy inside? Or have you ever observed children watching a parade? The wonder and delight they emote is contagious.

The reason why feelings spread so quickly is that human beings seek harmony and resonate with their environment. If there's a dominant energy in our space, we unconsciously tune in to it. It's similar to putting two guitars side by side and plucking a string on one of them—the same note will vibrate on the other instrument. This is called the "law of resonance."

We're like the guitars, only more so: We feel and respond to people's auric fields all the time, but most of us are usually unconscious of it. When we're around calm energy, we become tranquil; and when we're exposed to agitated vibrations, we can very easily become upset ourselves.

As you can see, energy fields are real, and they deeply affect us, especially kids. Have you ever noticed how quickly children react to someone who's being uptight? They can't stand it. They'll act out, become rude, or cower in the corner because the anxious person's energy makes them uncomfortable.

Consider the power of a mother's aura. If my mom was upset, we could feel it seeping out from under the front door before we even opened it. If she was out of sorts, she only had to walk into the room for her mood to have us in its grip. When we were growing up, our household anthem was "Happy mom, happy family." Her energy was so strong that we all felt what she felt, and so of course we wanted her to be cheerful. I sometimes wonder if everyone is affected by their mother's aura as much as we were. After talking to clients for years, I think the answer is yes.

Children who are raised in homes with violence, alcoholism, or a destructive environment manage to survive by perceiving psychic energy and learning how to either dodge it or improve it. However, they usually don't know they're doing so. The more sensitive kids languish and can become very withdrawn and sick if the atmosphere around them is extremely negative. Others cope by completely closing their hearts and tuning out their responsiveness to others. The problem is that it's hard to ignore what they feel—so difficult, in fact, that they sometimes resort to extreme measures and abuse drugs, alcohol, or even food in order to do so. These substances override their awareness and deaden their sensitivity, temporarily dulling the pain of disturbed family vibrations. Addiction is a sorry solution, but it does serve a purpose. Unfortunately, it also shuts down consciousness, self-esteem, empathy, creativity, and joy.

We need to pay very close attention to *how* other people's auric fields affect our children and ourselves so that we can take steps to prevent them from having a negative impact. So often, kids are subjected to someone else's highly unpleasant or detrimental energy, only to be shushed or ignored by the parent or authority at hand. Sometimes it's even the mom or dad who's giving off the toxicity. If young people are silenced, neglected, or exposed to bad vibes often enough, they'll begin to doubt their experience and shut down their awareness. And even then, the energy will still have an impact on them.

Aura Invasion

My client Dawn told me this story about her daughter Sharon, who met another little girl at camp one year who had an extremely unsettled aura and was competitive, jealous, and not very nice. Sharon played with her, but mostly because she was too sweet to object to this lousy treatment. She sucked it in all day, keeping her mouth shut as she took in the barbs, jabs, and manipulation— perhaps not fully understanding what was happening. But every afternoon, Sharon would come home with an aura filled with tension about the abuse she experienced at the hands of her new "friend." As soon as she was in her house where it was safe, she'd spew the toxic energy all over the place, making a terrible scene. She'd cry, act agitated, or start a fight with her younger brother. In fact, she'd display the same poor manners and disrespect that she'd endured all day long.

This went on for a month, and then Dawn called me for advice. I suggested that she help Sharon understand that she was picking up destructive vibes from the other child and that she needed to clear them.

Sharon responded to the idea enthusiastically, looking both intrigued and somewhat relieved that her mother had noticed that she needed help. "How do we do it, Mom?" she asked.

Dawn then shared what she'd learned from me. "Cleansing your aura is easy," she replied, "and it's useful when you've been around negativity, rudeness, hostility, or any energy that you simply don't like."

"In that case, I have to do it *every* day, because there's always someone bothering me at camp," Sharon said. Here are the techniques they used:

Establishing New Habits

— **Aura cleaning.** First, go outside (if the weather doesn't permit, use a quiet room). Stamp your feet on the ground (or better yet, jump up and down a few times) and draw in a deep, cleansing breath. Now turn your palms toward your body, about one to two inches away from your skin, until you feel the heat coming off of it. This is your aura, and it completely surrounds you, from the top of your head to below your feet. With your palms still facing inward, rub your hands over your energy field as though you were washing a windshield, and then shake them vigorously in the air.

Then imagine a loving white light pouring in at the crown of your head and settling in your heart. Visualize the light completely bathing your body, forming an egg-shaped field about six inches from your skin.

While doing this, begin to imagine everyone and everything that bothers you draining away from your aura and into the ground.

With your eyes closed, see whose face, if any, pops into your mind. If it's someone who has upset you, feel their energy flow away from you into the earth. Now picture a golden-white energy light replacing their vibration, infusing your heart and aura with peaceful feelings and casting a warm glow around your body.

Finally, inhale deeply as you imagine drawing energy up from the earth through the soles of your feet to the top of your head, filling your body and extending out beyond it for about five feet in all directions. Then exhale. That's it! Now you're completely clear.

Aura cleaning is a favorite after-school ritual in our house, and it's something kids often need to do, since, as any parent knows, their world can be just as toxic and unpleasant as an adult's. This cleansing ritual gives them a way to remove unwanted vibrations and reinforce their personal boundaries. It's useful when they've just failed a test, haven't been picked for the soccer team, are ignored by their best friend, or are the "odd man out" and aren't accepted by a play group. In short, it's an effective tool for healing all disappointments, letdowns, mistakes, failures, and upsets. It really does the job of clearing away harmful energy and helps your children restore their auric balance. (It will work for you, too!)

— **Sensing the aura.** You can help your kids become more conscious of negativity or unpleasant vibrations if you teach them to actually *feel* their auras. It's easy enough to do. Start by having your child place his feet solidly on the ground and find his center of balance. Then ask him to shake out his hands and breathe in very deeply. As he exhales, he needs to face his palms toward each other, about half an inch apart, in front of his chest. He should slowly move his hands in circles, close together but not touching. Ask him if he can feel any energy moving between his palms.

Do this exercise with him—you'll be delighted by the experience. You should both be able to sense the flow of energy passing gently between your hands. It will feel like "thick air" and may be warm or cool.

Next, ask him to close his eyes and continue to pull his palms away from each other until he can no longer feel the vibration between them. How far is this? Some kids can move their hands 18 to 20 inches apart before the sensation begins to fade. Now stand facing your child, turn your palms toward each other, and feel the energy passing between you—what you're experiencing is your aura!

If he can't feel his auric field while doing this exercise, another way to help him is to have him close his eyes and give him an extremely slow back rub. Then very gently lift your hands an inch or two away from his skin and stroke his energy field. Doing this a few times usually awakens sensitivity. Afterward, try the hand exercise again. If he still can't feel his aura, then forget about it—it doesn't really matter. Just knowing about it will heighten his awareness, whether he can sense it or not.

Our Auras Are Like Sponges

Explain to your children that the aura is like a sponge and can easily absorb the energy around other people and in the atmosphere. If they're around positive vibrations, they may soak them up; and in the same way, they may also take in any bad vibes they encounter. That's why it's vital not to let in any energy you don't want to *feel*.

It's also important to "squeeze out" any bad vibrations you may have picked up and replace them with clear, beneficial ones. Kids can do this by rubbing their hands together, running them through their energy field as if raking out debris, and shaking them off. This is a favorite technique of many massage therapists because it does the job well. You and your children can also practice this on each other.

Another way to cleanse your aura is through "grounding," which means literally connecting your awareness to the earth. Activities such as running, jumping, exercising, touching the dirt, hugging trees, or smelling flowers ground the energy in your body and pull out unwanted negativity.

Usually kids easily accept the notion of auras because they *do* feel them, even though they often don't have a name for what they're experiencing. Knowing how to sense and clear their energy fields will help protect them from bullies. For example, when she was younger, my daughter Sonia was very eager to grow up and liked to play with older children who could take advantage of her. One day, I said to her, "Honey, I know you enjoy doing things with these kids, which is fine with me, but you need to know how to keep from being pushed around."

"How can I, Mom? What should I do?"

"Well, anytime you begin to feel uncomfortable with a friend, you can always excuse yourself and tell him or her that you need to get some air. Then go outside, rub your hands together, shake off the vibrations, and pull in fresh energy from the earth."

"What if it's cold or snowing, or I'm at a sleepover?" she asked.

"Then go to the bathroom and shut the door. Shake off the bad energy, take a deep breath, and then wash your hands and face. If you ever get to the point where this doesn't help, just come home."

One of the most important things children learn in life is to set boundaries so that they won't be manipulated by others. Teaching them how to feel their auras, be aware of how other people's energy affects them, and clean away the vibrations that they don't like (or walk away at any time if they must) will give them tools for intuitive self-care.

Some parents ask, "Shouldn't we just prevent our kids from being exposed to negative people and circumstances?" Well, up to a point you can and should, but realistically, you can't possibly fend off every single harmful person or situation they may encounter before they're affected. Furthermore, trying to do this shields them from life itself and turns you into a control freak—which will only make your children resent you. It's much better to teach them about intuitive self-defense and how to identify trouble and move away from its source anywhere, at any time.

Personal Empowerment

My client Grace told me that since she introduced her son Everett to auras and showed him how to establish personal boundaries, he has become more and more conscious of how other people affect him. Now, at age 11, he can discern for himself whether someone's energy bothers him, and he freely moves away if he doesn't like what he's feeling. He has gradually stopped spending time with the kids who dominated him and has found more balanced friends he's comfortable with. He's making his own choices based on his awareness of how different people influence him.

Recently, for example, Everett had his first sleepover camp experience. During the week he was there, he felt irritated by one of the boys there. Everett didn't like his energy—which felt angry, unsettled, aggressive, and even dangerous—and would move away from him before they could even speak.

On the second-to-last day of camp, Everett had once again maneuvered away from the boy, who then picked up a large rock and, for no apparent reason, threw it at another unsuspecting child, striking her full force on the back. He started laughing, even though he'd really hurt her.

He was reprimanded and put on severe probation, which included not being allowed to go anywhere near the other kids for the rest of the day. His display of aggression was serious, and apparently it wasn't the first one, according to a counselor. He'd attacked another child the year before and had only been allowed to come back after much persuasion on the part of his parents.

Who knows why the boy was so hostile and aggressive—it wasn't Everett's job to figure that out, but he'd been right to avoid the child. Had his mom been clearing away the obstacles in his path all along, I wonder whether he'd have been able to choose to step away from danger on his own with as much awareness and determination. His mother was extremely happy to learn that he did have such a keen sense of his own boundaries, and it helped her rest easier as a parent.

Take Toxic Energy Outside

I've also taught my children to be aware of how their energy affects others—namely me! I've explained to them that fighting and squabbling, instead of trying to communicate, create toxic energy that I can't bear. I tell them that if they must quarrel, they have to do it outdoors and clear their auras before coming back in. Although this makes them mad, it also makes them conscious. They rarely want to take their differences outside, especially in cold weather, so they're more willing to negotiate their conflicts in a civilized fashion.

Of course, the same rules apply to Patrick and me. If we argue (and like all married people, especially those who live *and* work together, we do sometimes), we try to remember to be considerate enough to keep our negativity away from our daughters. If we forget, they have the right to remind us.

Disagreements are bound to arise in any home. This in itself is less of a problem than all the emotions that are discharged into a closed space during a heated discussion. The antagonism bounces around the room and settles into the atmosphere, preventing people from finding common ground or causing the fight to start all over again.

One way for you to resolve a dispute with a family member is to actually take it outside into the fresh air. Not only will the earth have a grounding, calming effect, but the disruptive energy will be dispersed into the environment rather than lingering in the corners and closets of your house.

The best protection you can offer your children is consciousness. Teaching them to be aware of their vibrations, love themselves, become selective about what they'll allow to affect them, and be proficient at clearing their energy will give them a few tools to keep themselves safe.

And one final word: While showing your kids how to become conscious of vibes and clear their auras is essential for balance, it can't take the place of counseling, therapy, or even medication if they're really feeling down or depressed or aren't engaging with the world in a positive way. Develop enough awareness of your children to sense the difference between a simple case of psychic pollution and a full-blown physical, emotional, or mental problem. In short, use your intuition and common sense when it comes to their well-being, and know when they need self-care tools or a skilled caretaker.

Establishing More New Habits

Here are some more tools for cleansing auras and setting personal boundaries:

— **Do the aura-cleansing stomp.** It's said that when you dance, your spirit fully descends into your body, bringing healing to every fiber and cell. Therefore, to clear your aura and energize your spirit, pick your favorite foot-stomping music. This can be rock 'n' roll, rockabilly, zydeco, hip-hop, reggae, disco, or Motown—any songs that are energetic, *happy,* and motivating will work. Turn up the volume as loud as the stereo (and you) can handle, and dance barefoot until you're ready to drop. This is a *very* soul-cleansing family activity that will release negativity and refresh you!

Practice this exercise a few times throughout the week, and pay attention to how it feels.

— **Wash it away.** An even better way to cleanse troubled energy is to take a salt bath—a technique I learned from my older sister Cuky, who's a massage therapist and trance healer. To do this, fill a tub to the top with hot water, and add three cups of Epsom salts. Have your child soak in it until the water cools down, and then rinse off in the shower. Breathe in and visualize white light filling your aura and then extending outward beyond your body in all directions for about five feet. Then exhale.

This is a fantastic way to eliminate negative vibrations as well as toxins in the body. In addition, its relaxing effect will bring on a wonderful night's sleep.

— **Walk it off.** Nothing clears an aura and calms negativity more effectively than a walk in nature. In fact, it's so helpful that you and your children should incorporate a short stroll into your daily routine. Even just going around the block twice is enough to drain away interference, eliminate psychic pollution, and restore clarity in your auric field.

— **Shake out your woolies.** As discussed in Chapter 6, the "woolies" are icky, irritable feelings. Kids can get them from being around people they don't like, riding the bus, or even just walking past an uncomfortable place. In fact, they can pick up woolies from any unpleasant atmosphere or situation; and it leaves them feeling anxious, restless, and uncomfortable. If your child has a bad case, try this exercise:

Ask her to jump up and down (preferably outside!) for one or two minutes. (Jump ropes are great for this.) Next, have her stand with both feet planted firmly together on the ground, with her eyes closed. Ask her to breathe very slowly and deeply and pretend that she's a tree. Tell her to imagine that the energy from the earth is climbing up through her roots, trunk, branches, leaves . . . and then on out into space. Guide her through the visualization one step at a time, reminding her to continue to breathe slowly in and out until she feels clear of all "wooly" feelings.

— **Picking up the pieces.** One of the hardest things for moms and dads is seeing their kids experience pain, disappointment, rejection, loss, or even cruelty. These upsets can come from mean playmates, insensitive teachers, or even irresponsible parents. Pride or fear often prevents young people from openly displaying their hurt feelings, but this doesn't mean that they aren't suffering or that they're all right. If you notice that your children have psychic or emotional wounds, try this exercise to help them recover their balance and inner joy:

Have them become quiet, close their eyes, and breathe deeply and slowly. Then ask:

- Where's your sadness? Have them point to or touch the area of their body that's holding the trouble.

- What color is it?

- What shape is it?

- How heavy is it? Let them compare it to something they can pick up or measure by weight.

Then tell your children: "Turn to your heart and ask your sadness what it wants." Let them tune inward and listen to what they need. Now say, "Together, let's send love and feelings to it so that you can feel happy again."

Next, rub your hands together and place them tenderly on their sad spot. Close your eyes and visualize a caring white light pouring through your palms into their wounded place. Ask the compassion of the Universe to move through you to help uplift their heavy heart.

Do this for one or two minutes (depending on how restless they are), asking them to breathe comfortably throughout the process and receive your love as you send it to them. Then gently remove your hands and give them a big hug and kiss, telling them that you love them.

— **Aromatherapy.** Using essential oils is another highly effective way to cleanse a child's aura. Lavender, bergamot, and chamomile are especially useful. Putting a drop on a pillow or a tiny bit in a bath can clear away toxic vibes and calm and soothe an agitated soul.

— **What color are you?** Yet another very revealing technique for checking kids' auras is to have them lie down on a large piece of paper (such as white butcher paper), and outline the shape of their body. Then give them a big box of crayons and have them color in their own energy field. If they choose bright, clear shades, then their aura is fine. However, if they use black, brown, or muddy colors, have them take an Epsom-salt bath, and put a little lavender on their pillow or in an aromatherapy diffuser in their room to help clear away psychic debris.

— **Back off, little buddy**. If you're in need of space and your children won't give it to you, gently but firmly explain to them that you need a little break to regain your energy . . . and then *take* it. Ask them to play quietly, read a book, or even watch TV while you rejuvenate yourself. They may balk at this suggestion or test you, but if you're truly determined to take a few moments for yourself without feeling guilt, even babies will intuitively sense your resolve and respect you.

Now sit down in a chair, close your eyes, put your feet flat on the floor, and inhale deeply. As you exhale, concentrate on quieting your mind. Find a steady rhythm and focus on breathing for a full five minutes. Don't rush through this centering exercise— a few minutes of peace will keep you patient and in harmony with your family, and everyone will be better off.

Reflections

- Have you felt your own aura? Are you becoming more conscious of your children's?

- Have you begun to teach your kids about their energy fields?

- Are you able to identify a toxic aura—your own, your family members', or other people's?

- Have you tried any aura-cleansing techniques? If so, which ones work best for you, and what do your children prefer? Do any of you feel different now that you've learned to clear away negative vibes?

- Have you asked your children whether they can see their etheric body or yours? If so, have them describe the colors (if they can't see it, they can say what color they *feel* it is). Ask yourself the same questions.

- Talk with your kids about auras and advise them to frequently "check in" with their own energy.

Reminders

Are you:

- Keeping your house clutter free and serene?
- Noticing the subtleties and tuning in to vibrations?
- Creating your own language of spirit?
- Remembering to clear your aura and your kids'?

Chapter Eight

BLIND SPOTS AND BAD HABITS

I constantly remind parents that developing an awareness of inner guidance is only one part of the equation for living an intuitive life. The other is having the willingness and flexibility to accept and respond to the sixth sense when it does show up. You and your children won't receive its value and benefits unless you can fully embrace its subtle messages and act accordingly. Intuition is a gift, but at times it may require that you change plans, break with tradition, rock the boat, challenge authority, or reverse your direction—and believe me, it often will.

Inner wisdom exists to help us make better decisions and prevent us from making costly or disruptive mistakes. It also serves to direct our attention to the best ways of achieving goals, alert us to potential problems and dangers, and protect us and keep us safely on our path. Therefore, it makes perfect sense that intuition—especially a child's—is likely to call for a change of plans.

This is a very important message for moms and dads because one of the greatest blocks to children's six-sensory awakening usually lies in the parents' unconscious or automatic inclination to tune out their kids' insights as a matter of habit.

For example, recently I was on a plane going from Minneapolis to Denver and was seated next to a well-dressed businessman and his six- or seven-year-old son. During the flight, the father took out *The Wall Street Journal* and began to read, while the boy, who sat between us, played with some sort of electronic game. I leaned back in my seat, deciding to meditate for a while.

A short time later, the child said, "Dad, I saw an angel in my room last night!" Hearing this, I opened my eyes.

Without even looking up from his paper, his father responded, "You were just dreaming."

There was silence, then a moment later his son spoke again, "No, I was awake, and she was in the corner just smiling at me."

The newspaper snapped as his dad turned the page and insisted, "There's no such thing. You were sleeping." And he continued to read.

The boy stopped playing his game but kept staring down at it. He took a breath and gave it one final try. "Dad, it was real. I was awake, and she was very beautiful."

Now the man seemed annoyed. "Son, this is nonsense! Now if you can put it out of your mind, we'll read a book together."

A puzzled look crossed the child's face, as if he were having an internal debate. Then he said, "Okay, let's do it." The father put his paper away, and they began to read.

My heart sank. The little boy had just made an extremely difficult decision. He'd had a wonderful spiritual experience and obviously wanted to share it with his dad, who had dismissed him without a thought. He'd also gotten his son to drop the subject in exchange for his full attention.

They read together for a while. The child was clearly enjoying interacting with his dad, but eventually the man got up and went to the bathroom. While he was gone, the boy picked up the electronic game and began to play once again.

Pondering how he was being cut off from his intuitive life, I impulsively leaned over to him and said, "You know what? I believe you *did* see an angel!"

With that, his whole face lit up. Then his father returned, and that was the end of our conversation.

What I witnessed on that flight is, sadly, very common. All too often, it only takes a dismissive remark from an insensitive or unaware parent to disconnect children from their inner knowing. As one woman put it, "If intuition were a fire . . . my mother would be a firefighter!"

Even those who are committed to encouraging the development of their kids' sixth sense can fall prey to negative responses. As human beings, we're all creatures of habit, especially when it comes to intuition; and some of our ingrained tendencies contain blind spots that interfere with our goals.

Intuition Is Real

One day my friend Julia recounted this story to me: Her daughter, Domenica, had just arrived home after a year away at college. Shortly after unpacking her bags, the young woman mentioned that she had a creepy feeling that someone was watching her. Julia dismissed it, thinking that she was simply unsettled after being away at school. After all, they lived on the outskirts of their small New Mexico town in a sparsely populated area.

The next evening Domenica came into her mom's bedroom, again saying that she had a terrible feeling she was being spied on. She asked whether Julia would mind if she slept with her that night. My friend saw that her daughter was really upset and moved over to make space for her in the bed, but she never once considered that there might indeed be a prowler around.

On the third night, Domenica, who was now chastising herself for being paranoid, went back to her own room and undressed for bed. In the reflection of her mirror, she saw a hooded man crouched outside the window, staring at her. She screamed loud enough to wake the dead, and her mother came running. The Peeping Tom ran off, and the women called the police.

The stranger had been observing Domenica for the past three days—and she wasn't the only one. Several people had reported him to the authorities during the same period. What alarmed Julia was that even though she'd been sensitive to her daughter's fears and more than willing to comfort her, she never once considered that Domenica's feelings might be valid.

"I wasn't *intending* to distrust or discount her intuition," Julia said. "I just did it automatically."

In another instance, my friend Carol told me a story about her son, Nile. She said that many years ago, when he was eight or nine years old and they were living in the country, their family dog, Bowser, disappeared. They were terribly upset and searched for him everywhere, but to no avail.

Five nights after Bowser went missing, Carol left Nile at home to attend an important dinner party. During the evening, he called Carol and said, "Mom, I hear some breathing outside, and I think it's Bowser. Can you please come home?"

"Nile, I honestly don't see how you could hear him when you're inside," she said. "You know we've looked everywhere. I think it's just your imagination. Please go back to bed."

A few days later, a hired hand from the farm next door came over to tell them that he'd found their dog lying next to the pipes through which pesticides were pumped into the irrigation system. The poison had puddled there, and Bowser had been drinking it. The saddest part was that if Carol had acted on Nile's information, perhaps the pet could have been saved.

Neither Julia nor Carol consciously discounted their children's intuition—they'd done so automatically. Their reactions stemmed from an ingrained culture that invalidates children's gut feelings (or anyone's, for that matter) without a second thought. As good mothers, they were more concerned about making the "bad" feelings go away than asking themselves what was behind them. They focused on reassuring their kids that all was well instead of considering that their children were messengers with important information.

Listen and Believe

Kids receive spontaneous six-sensory messages more readily than adults do; and as parents, we need to listen to them. After years of being indoctrinated to look for what the agenda calls for—for what *seems* to be instead of what *is*—our own intuitive edge begins to dull. In contrast, children usually have a pretty keen ability to discern what's what.

A good way to keep their instincts sharp, as well as reawaken your own, is to respect their first impressions, listen to their vibes, allow their natural responses, and encourage them to share their feelings with you. Take them seriously and believe what your kids are telling you, even if it seems unlikely or puts you in an uncomfortable or even awkward position.

A simple change in your awareness and habits in this area can create tremendous breakthroughs in sparking and validating your children's gifts, and also reactivate your own intuition. Pay attention to what they're saying, what they want to do, and what *you* want to do. If you recognize their vibes as an important response to energy, then you'll understand how a sensitive mind picks up these frequencies. In fact, a kid's clear mind can sense many things adults overlook or filter out because they don't want to know. Children do tune in to what we're tuning out, and they need you to show them that the information they're receiving matters.

Be Respectful

Last winter, out of the blue, Sabrina started complaining about being very scared to sleep on her own and begged me to let her stay in our room. After a few nights of this, I told her that I'd prefer that she go back to her own bed and that we needed to get to the bottom of her fears.

Tearfully she got under her covers and said, "I'm sorry, Mom. I don't know what the problem is! It's just that I have bad vibes."

I sat down beside her and tried to help her sort out her feelings. I've had hundreds of bad-vibe attacks myself, and they make me want to jump out of my skin, especially when my uneasiness is so vague that I don't have any idea what's causing it.

I decided to share an exercise that my mom used to do with me when I had similar experiences as a child. I focused my attention on her vibes and told her, "Sabrina, close your eyes, listen to your heart, and ask yourself what your worry is about. Can you sense who or what your feelings are about?"

"I don't know!" she cried, with her eyes shut. "I'm just worried that something could happen to one of us . . . maybe to Sonia or you."

"Well, Sabrina, if that's what your vibes tell you, we'd better say prayers and visualize white light surrounding all of us for protection," I answered.

She thought it was a great suggestion, and together we did just that. Then I massaged her feet for a few minutes to calm her down and stayed in her room until she fell asleep.

By the time I got to bed, it was late. This was the fourth night in a row that Sabrina had felt this way, and I have to admit that I wondered whether she was creating drama just to be the center of attention (which she was capable of doing), or if she really was getting a warning. But experience has taught me that it's always better to listen to and respect a vibe, no matter whose it is. As an added measure, I made a note to myself to keep a protective shield around all of us for the next couple of days.

When we woke up the next morning, the ground was covered in a beautiful, fresh blanket of snow. On the spur of the moment, Patrick and I decided to take the girls skiing in an area an hour away from our house. In the car, Sabrina mentioned her vibes one more time, and we all agreed that it meant we needed to be extra careful that day.

Once we got there, we had a splendid time. Patrick taught both of our daughters to ski when they were only three years old, so they were very comfortable on the slopes, and we were all relaxed. However, after a while, as Sonia and I approached the chairlift, we noticed that it was going faster than it had been. Before we were ready, a seat flew up behind our legs and scooped us up. Sonia's skis got tangled, and she suddenly slipped off and fell a few feet to the ground. She popped her head up as soon as she landed.

"Get down!" I screamed at her, and instantly she dived back down as the oncoming chair just missed hitting the back of her head.

The chairlift operator slammed off the machine and dragged Sonia over to the side as I jumped off the lift and stumbled over to her. A bit bruised, we limped off to the lodge, shaken but relieved that we'd avoided a terrible accident.

Once inside, hot chocolate in hand, Sonia asked me, "Do you think this is what Sabrina was picking up on?"

I nodded. We decided that since we were all right, we wouldn't ruin the fun for Patrick and Sabrina by telling them about the incident until later. When we shared what had happened on the way home, Sabrina's eyes popped open as she exclaimed, "So that's what I was feeling!"

We'll never know for sure, but it's a fact that Sabrina slept soundly that night without any fuss at all.

Bad Vibes and Bad News

Sometimes kids get bad vibes about the people we're the least suspicious of. They may even be friends or family members. We adults may have a hard time believing that someone we know and like isn't really safe to be around.

One of my clients, Ron, recounted a frustrating experience he'd had as a teenager, when he got a bad feeling about Jim, the husband of his mom's best friend, Irene. Jim had been married to Irene for a long time and was considered a good friend of the family.

When Ron was 11 years old, Jim started visiting the family while on business trips each year. To all appearances, he was a nice, easygoing guy, but Ron could never really let his guard down around him. Although he couldn't put his finger on exactly what the problem was, he kept his distance. Ron's younger brothers, nine-year-old Sam and ten-year-old Howie, loved Jim and didn't share Ron's suspicions, in spite of his warnings to "watch out" every time the man came to their house.

One summer when Jim was visiting, he started wrestling with Howie in the yard, and after a few minutes pinned him to the ground. Ron was watching from the back porch and became extremely upset. He ran over and ferociously pulled Jim off Howie, screaming, "Get off of him *right now!*"

Jim, Howie, and Ron's mother and father (who'd heard the yelling) looked at him as if he'd gone crazy. He was given a serious lecture for being so rude and was sent to his room.

"I'll never forget the moment when I yanked Jim off my brother," Ron says. "Our eyes locked for an instant, and then he looked away. That was Jim's last visit, and he lost touch with us after that."

A few years later, when Ron was 16, he came home from school one day and was met by his mom, who had an odd look on her face.

"I got a surprising call from Irene today," she said. "She told me that Jim was arrested. Apparently he molested a neighborhood kid. We're *so* shocked!"

Ron threw his books on the floor. "Son of a gun! I *tried* to tell you he was weird, but you guys wouldn't listen to me."

"It's true," she said. "You sensed something we didn't."

Ron told me that his parents apologized that day, grateful that Jim hadn't hurt him or his two brothers.

Believe it or not, my client's experience isn't uncommon. I've talked to hundreds of people who say that when they were children, they had bad vibes about someone; and instead of being listened to, they were completely ignored or quickly dismissed and sometimes even punished for suggesting that anything could be wrong. When kids have intimations of danger or dishonesty, parents can easily slip into one of several responses. One is to "shoot the messenger," as Ron's mom and dad did. Another is to try to change their child's negative feelings. This happens when the parents like the person in question and don't want to hear any more about it.

Raining on the Parade

My friend Renee gave me another example of how parents can discount their kids' intuition. As a single mother raising her only child, Laura, who was six years old, Renee didn't have much of a love life, so she was delighted when she met a man she really clicked with. According to her, Fred was a perfect gentleman and was easygoing, yet Laura didn't like him.

At first, Renee suspected that her daughter felt competitive and that in time she'd change her mind about him . . . but she didn't.

Renee told her how kind he was and how much she enjoyed his company, but it didn't work—Laura still didn't like Fred.

Finally, the exasperated mom decided that the girl was just being stubborn and chose to ignore her, because she was interested in Fred, which was all that mattered to her at the time. She continued to see him and was very excited about a possible future with him. Renee was in love!

However, after another month passed, Renee received a call at work from Fred's wife! She couldn't believe he was married. When she confronted him, he finally admitted the truth.

"All I could think about was how Laura had been right all along," my friend told me. "Fred wasn't as he appeared, and she'd felt it. I told her I was sorry that I'd so readily discounted her. I'd believed what I wanted to, while Laura stuck with what was *true*.

"When I later met Herb, Laura liked him right away. She laughed at his jokes, didn't mind when he came over, and even teased us when we went out on dates. We've been married for three years now, and I feel we're a real family."

As was the case for Ron's parents and Renee, it can be very easy to shut down or deny our sensory awareness (or someone else's) when we want to believe the best about a person. Perhaps because they're so little and depend so heavily on adults for protection, kids usually have their instincts set on "high." So, I think that we should never ignore any of their vibes.

My friend Phyllis once said to me, "But it's hard to know what to believe when they're young. So much of what they say is just imagination."

"True," I replied, "but *all* intuition arises out of the imagination. It's better to pay attention to everything than to dismiss something and regret it later."

Acknowledging children's bad vibes is one way to keep them—and often yourself—out of harm's way. Kids who are grounded and confident that they'll be listened to with respect when they express themselves are usually avoided by creeps and opportunists. As my teachers taught me, "Acceptance and respect are the highest forms of protection in life."

Better Safe Than Sorry

My friend Amy told me a story about an intuitive experience she had as a child that caused a lot of commotion. When she was three years old, her family visited her grandparents in Michigan, and her parents bought a secondhand Oldsmobile from them. The plan was that they'd drive it back home to Long Island.

As soon as they'd loaded the vehicle and were on the road, Amy began to act out. She was never one to throw a tantrum, so this behavior was very unlike her. She kicked and screamed that she hated the car and refused to settle down. This went on for some time and began to upset her parents, especially since her other four siblings were dozing off.

Finally, Amy's mother insisted that her husband pull into a service station so they could try to calm Amy down. She took her daughter to the bathroom and attempted to get her to relax a bit, but to no avail. Amy yelled again that she hated the Oldsmobile and threw herself down on the ground, refusing to move.

Amy's father was out of patience and tried to pull her up, but his wife suddenly stopped him. She knew this behavior was absolutely out of character for the girl, and her own intuition told her that perhaps there was something wrong. She requested that he have the car checked out to see if indeed anything might be malfunctioning, so he asked the service-station attendant to have a look—anything to stop the scene and get going.

Much to their shock, the man found a hole the size of a silver dollar in the fuel line, which was causing carbon monoxide to leak into the interior. That explained why Amy's three sisters and brother had fallen asleep so quickly.

"If you'd carried on for another few hours, you might have all been dead," the attendant said in a most dramatic fashion. "Thank God you noticed! What a miracle!"

All eyes were on Amy, only now they were filled with complete amazement and appreciation.

Is it a hassle to pay attention to kids' intuition? It can be—but it's not nearly as bad as the consequences of ignoring them! This doesn't mean that you should become hypervigilant; that kind of attention would be unnatural and make them uncomfortable. Simply listen to your children if they do express uneasiness about anything. And if they have bad vibes, let them know that you're paying attention to what they feel is important and will do what you can to change the situation if necessary.

Getting Familiar

There's a difference between bad vibes and simply protecting ourselves with natural reserve. We all start out in life with six senses, including our intuition. One of its functions is keeping us out of harm's way. It scans our environment and alerts us to anything that's different from our own energy field.

In children, novel vibrations elicit this natural reserve. When they encounter a new person or situation, they must first familiarize themselves with the strange energy before they'll open up. This is why babies, for example, turn their eyes away when a stranger looks too closely at them. If they feel that the individual's vibes are friendly, they may gradually steal a peek their way. Otherwise, they may simply avoid eye contact. As they adjust to the energy and become more comfortable, they naturally open up to new people or environments—in their own time, at their own pace.

My very outgoing friend, Alan, has a two-year-old daughter named Jennifer. He greets everyone with a smile, while she runs behind his leg and peers out. He's constantly encouraging her to come out and say hello, especially in elevators. I suggested that he stop doing so, since it isn't instinctive for two-year-olds to address strangers. Alan's coaxing was scrambling Jennifer's innate boundaries and causing her unnecessary anxiety.

When parents interfere and push their children to communicate with unfamiliar people before they're ready, they override the natural responses of their kids, who then lose touch with their inner guidance. When this happens, they become very vulnerable. It's no wonder that they grow into adults who ignore their gut feelings and simply go along with appearances, which often leads to trouble later in life. If we become disconnected from our instincts, we can end up associating with individuals who don't have our best interests at heart—and not realize it until it's too late, as in the case of the business partner who takes advantage of us or the friend who betrays us.

Another mixed message we give our kids often relates to what constitutes polite behavior. When we take them to visit friends or relatives, we say "Give Aunt Mary a kiss" or "Give Uncle Joe a hug," only to have our children recoil or resist, embarrassing us and making them feel rude.

The truth is that spontaneous affection with strangers, even those we're related to, is highly unnatural; and the intuitive instinct to refrain from such forced intimacy is quite correct. We need to assess a person's energy and discern whether or not we're at ease with it before we open ourselves up. This is true for ourselves and even more so for children. After all, as kids, they're more vulnerable than adults and consequently *need* to be more cautious.

Therefore, respect their natural boundaries and offer more comfortable and self-respecting ways to be polite. A simple "Say hello to so-and-so" is just as courteous and much more appropriate than insisting on an unwanted hug.

It takes attention and sensitivity to remember that children are much more honest and relaxed about creating an energetic balance than we give them credit for. All it takes is a little creativity and common sense on our part to make whatever adjustments are necessary in any given situation. It's much easier to do so if we remember that our intuitive requirements, and those of our kids, are just as real and important as our needs for food, water, and oxygen. They shouldn't require any more debate than these basics do.

Speak for Yourself

I know a woman who has several children and loves them greatly, but every time we visit a curious thing happens. I might ask the oldest, who's 11 years old, "How are you, Lucy?" But before the girl can even open her mouth, her mom chimes in, "Oh, she's just fine, thank you. Aren't you, Lucy?"

And then her daughter will smile and stand there passively. Or I'll ask, "How is school this year?" and her mother pipes up, "Terrific! She's having a great time. Isn't that right, dear?" And the child just nods, with her eyes on Mom.

I know that this mother is only attempting to teach the art of conversation, but in answering for her child, what she's really communicating is a vote of no confidence in Lucy's ability to respond and express herself. Or perhaps her mom doesn't want her to share anything she's unhappy about. It's also possible that this woman's need to present a perfect picture to the world has shut down Lucy's capacity to experience and show her true feelings. Maybe it's a habit her mom learned as a child herself. Who knows?

All I'm certain of is that when it comes to emotions, rather than checking in with herself, Lucy defers to her mother. It's as if she's saying, "Mom, tell me how I feel about that question." This could lead to real problems in the future. At age 11, she has already abandoned her own feedback system and is disconnected from her intuition.

Be patient with your children when they're trying to share their feelings and allow them the room they need to get in touch with themselves when you engage them in a conversation. Realize that when kids are asked, "How are you?" they usually believe the question is sincere, and therefore are inclined to take a moment to reflect before answering. It's often in this pause that an enthusiastic parent chimes in with a response, feeling uncomfortable with the momentary silence.

Exercising a little patience when talking to children—especially adolescents—usually reaps great rewards for both you and them. It allows you to connect with them in more than a superficial way, and it lets them know that their feelings are important because you're taking the time to listen to them.

Bad Vibes vs. Fear of the Unknown

Just as there's a difference between bad vibes and natural reserve, there's also a distinction between them and a normal fear of the unknown, which is part of our innate system of checks and balances. It slows us down and heightens our awareness when we're exposed to potential danger, and it's our most basic survival instinct.

J. J. Bittenbinder, a Chicago detective who hosts the television show *Tough Target,* calls our fear of the unknown the "hairs standing up on the back of your neck" syndrome, and says it's what keeps us alive as a species. A good example of this is when we wander all alone down an unfamiliar, dark street at night. Even though it may not necessarily be harmful, it *could* be. Therefore, it's very likely that we'll have a healthy dose of the "fear of the unknown" coursing through our veins—just in case.

This particular instinct vacillates in intensity, depending upon the situation. The more vulnerable we are, the more intensely afraid we may be. That's why some kids—especially those who are abandoned, neglected, or live in violent conditions—are extremely anxious. They're in danger, and their heightened fear, by making them hypervigilant, may save their lives.

Most of the time, however, children's dread of the unknown isn't based as much on a physical threat as on a psychic upset brought about by being placed in unfamiliar circumstances or by conditions that cause emotional vulnerability—such as when they're invited to visit a new friend for the first time, when they need to visit the dentist, or when they're changing schools. Although these aren't dangerous situations, kids nevertheless find themselves in ungrounded and isolating energy that leaves them feeling nervous, vulnerable, and scared.

A client's eight-year-old daughter, Louise, even experienced this type of anxiety when she was given a brand-new bed. "I'm scared to sleep in it, Mommy," she said. "It doesn't *feel* safe . . . like it isn't mine!" It took her two weeks before she was comfortable enough to fall asleep easily.

I've seen parents become very annoyed and impatient with their children when they become afraid in obviously nonthreatening situations. A father once said to me, "My daughter is just overreacting. She needs to get over it and discover new things."

"Yes, she does," I agreed. "Yet the truth is that even though children should expand their horizons, it doesn't change the fact that, energetically, it *can* feel overwhelming and scary for them."

If your children get worried about unfamiliar things or situations, instead of saying "There's nothing to be afraid of," try offering a few understanding words to acknowledge their anxiety. After all, even adults can become nervous when entering uncharted waters in life, so why be surprised or insensitive when children react the same way?

You can calm kids' fears in several ways. The first is to ask them to identify, to the best of their ability, why they're distressed. Sometimes, simply encouraging them to do so reduces their worries and helps them put the situation into perspective. Another method is to suggest that they visualize themselves surrounded by a loving white light, protected by God and His angels. Knowing that they're in such a safe cocoon greatly helps insecure children become more grounded and at ease. It also reminds them that as spiritual beings, they're never truly alone and that the Universe is gently watching over them at all times.

You may also want to try some of the aura-clearing and energy-grounding techniques that we discussed in Chapter 7, such as the Aura-Cleansing Stomp or Picking Up the Pieces. These tools and rituals are great for the "I want to go . . . I don't want to go!" ambivalent moments in life when kids' desires collide with their fears!

The best way to handle their anxieties about the unknown is to be patient, matter-of-fact, and respectful and to listen to what they're feeling (and fearing). Don't overreact or attempt to deny what they're experiencing in an effort to make them feel better. Be especially careful not to call their worries "nothing." It might not be anything that's physical or that you can feel, but it's *something* energetic and is very real to them.

Calmly ask them what their vibes feel like and if there's anything they want you as a parent to do. Once they respond, see if they can be more specific, using prompts such as "I know you don't care for our family friend. Is there anything in particular you don't like?" or "I know you're afraid to go to Sue's house today. Is there something specific you're worried about?"

This type of focused questioning will help your child separate vague anxieties from real danger, and it reminds them that you're supportive and sensitive to their psychic state and are willing to protect them and keep them safe in the world.

Fear of the Dark

Another common variant of the "dread of the unknown" syndrome is fear of the dark. Many children become terrified of it and can't go to sleep unless the lights are on, convinced that the "boogeyman" or some other creature of the night is waiting to get them.

My client Jeff came to see me because he was greatly frustrated that his seven-year-old son, Kyle, was scared of the dark. The child was petrified by it and absolutely refused to sleep without the lights on and the door open. Because they lived in a small two-bedroom apartment, this requirement was keeping his parents up all night. Exhausted, Jeff was running out of patience with Kyle and his nighttime needs.

"How do I get him to stop this nonsense?" my client asked. "I've explained to him a thousand times that there's nothing lurking in his room, but he won't believe me. It's all I can do to keep from losing my temper with him."

"To begin with, you can stop telling him there's *nothing* there," I said. "There may not be something physical, but Kyle is definitely feeling some sort of unsettled energy. It would be far more soothing and reassuring to explain to him that what he's sensing is a little bit of disrupted but harmless energy left over from the day, which is *something* but not *someone*. Also tell him that when the lights are out, he becomes more sensitive to it. Then offer to do an energy-clearing ritual to calm his bedroom, such as smudging or saying a prayer. Surround Kyle with a protective white light and even invite his angels into his room to watch over and protect him during the night. Doing this helps in two ways: First, it shows him that you take his feelings seriously; and second, it actually *does* clear the environment of any lingering and undesirable vibrations so that he can sleep better."

"Hmm . . . I never considered taking him seriously," said Jeff. "We've tried everything else and it has failed, so I guess we've got nothing to lose. Frankly, as tired as I am of all this, I'm willing to try anything!"

Jeff took my suggestion, and that night before bedtime, he, his wife, and Kyle said a prayer, asking that his son's guardian angel cleanse the room of any negativity and fill it with a protective white light. Then they burned a smudge stick as an added measure "to clear away the old stuff," as the little boy put it.

Kyle was delighted with their efforts but still wanted the lights on. After a few more reassuring words, he finally agreed to leaving a dim night-light on instead—"so the angels can see better," his mom said. They also left the bedroom door open.

Happy with the results of these negotiations, Kyle hopped in bed; and to Jeff's amazement and great relief, he was fast asleep in 15 minutes. Ten minutes later, so were his mom and dad.

"I don't know if it was the prayer, the smudge stick, the psychological attention, or the love we showered on him, but by golly, it worked!" a more rested Jeff exclaimed when he called two days later.

"All of the above, I'm sure!" I answered.

Easy Does It

Even though many parents err on the side of underplaying intuition's role in their children's lives, another group of enthusiastic mothers and fathers goes a bit overboard and makes too much of a fuss over it. That's very annoying to kids and will shut off their sixth sense just as readily as ignoring them will.

My client Holly showed up at my door one day with a three-page list of observations about her three-year-old son Tim's intuitive abilities. She was sure that every little word out of his mouth was evidence of great insight. She coached, coaxed, prodded, and hovered over him, interpreting all of his responses as deep, meaningful revelations.

"Sonia, he stared at the babysitter for three whole minutes before he said hello," she reported. "It was as if he were reading her every inner secret. Whenever we're around new people, I ask Tim what color their aura is and what he's feeling. Do you think he's six-sensory?"

Of course I *did* think so, and I thought Holly had the right idea to nurture his ability, but her hovering over him, waiting for a sound-and-light show, was definitely the wrong approach. It was unnatural and awkward, as well as an invasion of her son's space. Any kid would certainly have sensed and resented such pressure.

Children don't enjoy being treated as "different," either in front of people or behind closed doors. They expend a great deal of energy trying to fit into society, not to be singled out. Even though it's just as important for parents to cultivate their kids' intuitive perceptions as it is to help them appreciate music or art, it's neither helpful nor desirable to make them self-conscious—no child likes that. And if a mom or dad approaches their little ones' vibes too seriously, it takes the fun out of it as well.

You'll never spark intuition through coercion, demands, testing, or obsessing. Such manipulation only engages their ego, completely bypassing the soul. The ego doesn't have access to intuition—only Spirit does—so this kind of behavior will never make the connection that you want. However, when you listen, you engage children's essence, capture their souls, and tap into their spirits.

The most effective approach you can take is to gently appreciate your kids' intuition as a part of the chemistry that makes them who they are. Allow them to discuss every aspect of their inner life freely, without pressuring them, being dramatic, or treating their abilities as something unusual, because this will make them feel nervous and compelled to live up to your expectations. Any overreaction is death to a budding sixth sense and will only create codependency instead.

Check your own attitude. At this point, you should begin to understand that we're all thinking, feeling, sensing, and intuitive beings, and our psychic lives are just as important an aspect of our magnificent makeup as our eyes and ears. Relax, allow room for exploration and discovery, and trust that your kids' higher awareness will flourish naturally without your having to control it.

Everything Counts

In summary, the most important thing to learn about responding to your children's gut feelings is to not shoot the messenger or let sentimentality cloud your perspective. If they have warnings, heed them. If they express disturbances, honor them. If they show dislikes, respect them. If they need space, give it to them. If they're fearful, be sensitive and reassuring. And do all of this *lovingly.* Clear minds pick up clear vibes, and kids do have an uncannily keen sense of the obvious, so recognize their intuitive messages as an attempt to stave off problems, keep their balance, and warn or protect themselves and you—and appreciate them for it.

Whatever you do, don't make them feel as though they're the cause of any vibes—whether good, bad, or indifferent. This is unfair, unkind, and untrue.

It's important to wake up and smell the coffee if you aren't paying attention! Take off the rose-colored glasses if you wear them. Snap out of denial if you're in it, and change your plans when you're called to. Be glad that your children are using all their senses to keep life safe, balanced, and honest.

The good thing about recognizing and honoring their vibes, natural boundaries, heightened instinct for self-preservation, and keen sense of the obvious is that you can't help but become sensitive to your own inner guidance as well.

In a power-and-control culture such as ours, we've all been highly indoctrinated to "go with the program" without question, but doing so often runs counter to listening to our hearts and doing what's right for ourselves. Intuition is a gift from Spirit, but it's still up to us to reach out and accept the treasure when it's offered— even though at times it may disrupt our plans, challenge authority, or make us reevaluate people and perspectives we're attached to.

It takes courage to act on the messages of the heart and believe in the wisdom of the soul, but the rewards are worth the effort.

Breaking out of unconsciousness and automatic habits and following the guiding winds of Spirit—whether arising in your child or yourself—no matter what the consequences are, is the turning point in living an intuitive life. The day that you decide to do so, your life and your children's will open to the light and abundant gifts of God's grace.

Establishing New Habits

If you *really* want your children to trust their intuition, you'll have to do so first. If you place enough value on what their instincts tell them, so will they. Try the following:

1. Listen to your kids with an open mind.

2. Become aware of their signals and communications.

3. Allow them to speak freely.

4. Respect their vibes and instincts.

5. Focus on your children's body language and offer protection.

6. Be patient when they voice their inner feelings, especially when they're inconvenient, upset your plans, or point to something negative in someone close to you.

7. Have humor and flexibility when intuition arises.

8. When in doubt, always trust a child's gut feelings— and yours, too, for that matter.

9. Don't look for trouble, but don't ignore your kids' bad vibes or your own when they appear.

10. Urge everyone in the family to speak up when it comes to intuition.

Reflections

• Are you willing to respect your children's natural boundaries and first impressions?

• Do you unconsciously impose rules of politeness that override their gut instincts?

• Are you too busy to incorporate their intuition into your decisions?

• Do you tune your kids out when their insights cause you to feel uncomfortable?

• Are you in such a chronically negative emotional state—anxious, harried, or angry—that you're out of touch with your child's vibes or your own?

Reminders

Are you:

• Creating your own language of spirit?

• Remembering to clear your aura and your kids'?

• Being respectful of all vibes, however inconvenient or unpleasant they may be?

You've already learned a lot about awakening intuition and creating a supportive environment that will encourage your children to trust their vibes. Now you can take the next step and discover ways to ask your soul directly for the guidance you desire.

✳   ✳   ✳

PART III

Asking for Support

Hurray! We're moving into the final phase of nurturing an intuitive family: asking for support. In Part III, you'll concentrate on shifting your focus from merely being aware and accepting the sixth sense to actively seeking its counsel in your life. You'll do this by:

1. Creating an atmosphere of wonder and discovery

2. Using art as a way to reach the intuitive heart

3. Introducing your children to the importance of asking for guidance

4. Meeting your angels, helpers, and guides

5. Finding ways to encourage your kids to turn inward and expect direction from their soul during their quiet time

6. Learning that the body is temporary, but the soul is eternal

You and your children are about to move from a life that's ordinary, ego based, and fearful to one that's extraordinary, spiritually directed, and secure. Continue your efforts, knowing that soon you and your family will reclaim the guiding wisdom of your souls!

✹ ✹ ✹

Chapter Nine

CREATING AN ATMOSPHERE OF WONDER AND DISCOVERY

I was talking last week with my friend Bill, who has just recently reclaimed his intuitive voice after a long silence. In describing his experience, he said, "It's like discovering a muscle you didn't know you had—first you have to find it, and then you have to use it!"

It's true. Developing your inner awareness is like strengthening a part of your body. At first you may resist or it may feel odd. But with practice, your vibes get stronger and stronger, and you become more comfortable tuning in to them. Intuition is a subtle feeling, a quick flash of "Aha!" and the lightbulb going on in your head. It's the "I just *feel* it, however faintly" sensation that flits by like a feather brushing your cheek, and all of us have experienced it a million and one times.

But as so many upstanding members of the "woulda-coulda-shoulda" club of intuitive hindsight will testify, knowing something and having the *confidence* to act on it are two entirely different things. As Bill put it, "It's hard to go with your gut feeling sometimes. You get so scared of making a mistake that it paralyzes you." And he's right—it *can* be unnerving. The reason why is that all too often we demand perfection of ourselves.

The best way to avoid blocked intuition is to learn *how* to use our psychic muscles freely and without censure or harsh consequences when we're growing up. The fear of doing something wrong that Bill mentioned actually settles in during childhood. This is the time when kids are either encouraged to explore and are allowed the opportunity to goof up without dire results, or are penalized for their errors and become too afraid to take any chances. How your children feel about taking risks, especially intuitive ones, is largely determined by you.

If you're extremely goal oriented, evaluate your self-worth by your performance, and don't tolerate slipups, then chances are that your kids will also strive for success in the same way in order to gain your approval. This kind of upbringing creates extremely anxious children, making it very tough for them to access their intuition, because whenever we're afraid, our distress overrides our inner voice or completely drowns it out. As a result, we grow up listening to our fears instead of our heart.

I've noticed that an alarming number of ambitious baby boomers are driven by the need for their children to be the best—and not in the areas in which they have natural talents, but in those where the *parents* think they should excel. They push, cajole, threaten, and even demand that their sons and daughters become top performers.

I've seen kids as young as six or seven years of age comparing themselves to one another based upon their grades, extracurricular activities, or how well they play a musical instrument. I know a gifted piano teacher who has permanently canceled recitals because of the competition, aggression, and fear of failure her students display during performances. "You can be sure it's the parents causing all their stress," she says. "Kids don't act like this naturally—they *learn* to."

With so many children carrying the burden of their parents' expectations and ambitions on their small shoulders at younger and younger ages, it's no wonder that fear becomes their guiding voice. The best way to ensure that your kids grow up motivated by a strong sense of inner direction rather than extreme anxiety is to create as many avenues as possible for them to flex their intuitive muscles. This means fostering a sense of play, adventure, discovery, and wonder. You need to allow them to awaken their sixth sense through delightful opportunities where they can experiment with what they really enjoy and express what they feel without risk of censure or failure—or worst of all, the loss of your love.

The "I Wonder" Game

Because intuition operates most powerfully in the realm of the imagination, the best way to access it is through creative play. When I was very young, my family had lots of kids and little money. We lived on a lean budget, but my mother had an incredible knack for turning the ordinary into the extraordinary and transforming everyday events into special moments. One of the ways she did this was teaching us a fun activity called *I Wonder*. She used to tell us, "*Wonder* is a magic word, and when you use it, you play with the Universe!" *I Wonder* was like a guessing game, only we weren't just randomly choosing answers—we actually were practicing tapping into our intuition.

When the phone rang, my mom would say, "I wonder who it could be. Don't you?" And we'd close our eyes and muse: *Is it Dad? Is it Mom's best friend, Charlotte? Is it Grandma?* Then we tried to *feel* who it was. We had a great time sending our minds on such delightful adventures. We'd each take a turn naming the caller before we picked up the receiver. When we found out who it was, we'd cheer ourselves on if we'd been right or laugh if we'd been wrong. It didn't matter—after all, it was just a game.

We had more *I Wonder* opportunities at the grocery store: *I wonder what's on special today? I wonder which apples are the best? I wonder what Dad wants for dinner?* In fact, this practice became part of our lives. We'd wonder what the school lunch was, when the pop quizzes were coming, and what the answers were. It was a natural way of navigating through the day.

I've been wondering since I was a little girl, and it has opened my eyes and pointed me in the right direction thousands of times. The best part is that it has helped me approach situations with a receptive mind and heart. Growing up being curious and asking questions shaped how I do everything today. It's a hard habit to break because it's so enjoyable, and it makes life work better.

It helps when you wonder who people really are instead of judging by appearances. It's also useful when you explore the best way to do a job instead of falling into a rut. Above all, wonder directs your attention to options that you might otherwise have overlooked, and it keeps your awareness fresh and keen.

You can play *I Wonder* with kids of any age. It teaches them to explore the unseen world with the same enthusiasm that they give to their physical surroundings. In addition, it encourages them to access the unknown, spiritual, and intuitive aspects of life and of themselves. And the best part is that it's fun!

You can enjoy the game anywhere, anytime. It works well in any situation, but it's best when a child is wondering about something he or she is really interested in. Sonia wonders on the piano, trying to play songs she's enjoyed hearing on the radio. Sabrina wonders how to draw objects and people from ancient times. We all wonder where our keys, shoes, backpacks, and coats are from time to time; and we have a ball letting curiosity guide us.

When playing the game, there are several rules to follow: The first is that you can't be wrong because it's not a test. If you let it become one, it loses its magic. Second, when you're not right or go off course, you just say, "Oh well!" and laugh—and then wonder some more. That way, there are no negative consequences to worry about. And the last rule is that when you come up with a positive solution or outcome, you celebrate—a lot!

Encourage your kids to play *I Wonder* early in life. Lay out the rules clearly, and when they break them (and you can count on this happening, because competition is everywhere!), help them back off and regroup. Introduce the activity whenever you can and invite them to share their ideas about fresh ways to wonder. This is a marvelous route to access inspiration, insight, creativity, and intuition; and it will support your family in staying open to new experiences.

A Sense of Adventure

Another way to develop intuitive muscles is to introduce a sense of adventure into your family life through travel. Patrick and I are avid globe-trotters, and whenever we can, we take our children with us. It introduces them to new situations, customs, food, and people; shows them that there are many different ways to live; and fosters curiosity and an open mind. It also heightens awareness, sharpens their instincts, turns their sensory apparatus on high, and usually jump-starts the intuition, which thrives on novel or unfamiliar environments. Parents are now traveling with kids in record numbers, and are even taking them out of school to do so. To this I say, "Terrific!"

My own intuition went from moderately activated to full-blown knowing when I had my first big adventure at the age of 16. Having always been fascinated by Romania, where my mother was born, and knowing that her family (who'd been separated from her during World War II) had eventually been found, I wanted to discover who they were. I asked my mom if she'd take me to meet her brothers and sisters if I bought my own ticket. Impressed with my ambition, she agreed. "If you earn the money, we'll go," she said.

I worked two jobs after school, one in an ice-cream parlor and the other in a gift shop. It took me nine months, but I did manage to save $817 for a round-trip Denver/Bucharest ticket. We left on October 17, 1976. In the end, my oldest sister, Cuky, a flight attendant, also joined us.

Arriving in Bucharest was like landing on the moon for me. Everything was so different from Denver, and because it was such a contrast, my sixth sense was working overtime.

One morning I woke up and told my mom, "I have a strong feeling we'll meet your godmother . . . I think I dreamed about it." At the time, I didn't even know she had a godmother! My mother replied, "Sonia, she must be dead. She's got to be more than 90 years old."

Later that day, my uncle took us for a drive. We entered a village and stopped at the cemetery where my grandparents were buried. After visiting their graves, we left in a somber mood. My Uncle Costel, a bright and exuberant person, reached over and touched my mom's elbow. "Now surprise!" he said cheerfully in his very basic English.

He led us down the road about 200 yards to a spot where a very, very old lady was sitting on a bench. My uncle said something to my mother in Romanian, and she threw her arms up in shock. She turned to me and exclaimed in astonishment, "My God, Sonia, you were right! This is my godmother."

A strange feeling of awe and satisfaction flushed over me. It was one of the most important affirming moments of my life.

Sometimes people say to me: "Travel is great, but what if you can't do it? What if you don't have the money or time to get away?" I maintain that you can always find ways to have an adventure if you really want to. An overnight camping trip or a day's excursion to a neighboring city are good ways to start. Use your imagination, for it all begins there. And if you're truly unable to go anywhere, there are other creative ideas for traveling with your children.

I know a woman named Grace who has raised a highly intuitive and imaginative son. She told me: "When I was a young single mother in New York, living from paycheck to paycheck, Adam and I had dinner in a foreign country every Sunday. First we'd choose a place, and then his assignment was to learn what he could about it, while mine was to prepare one of its traditional meals. During the week, I'd go to the store, and he'd go to the library; and on Sunday, we'd meet at the dining table. By the time he moved out, we'd been all over the world together, and each trip cost only the price of dinner for two."

At the time, Adam used the encyclopedia as the source of his explorations. Now, kids with access to a computer can go even further. They only need a sense of adventure, which fosters curiosity and is an essential fuel for the engine of intuition.

Travel and exposure to new experiences are becoming even more important because an increasing number of children are growing up in sequestered and isolated suburban communities where a homogenized culture filters out variety. If all of the families your kids are exposed to have essentially the same lifestyle, background, skin color, values, and opinions, their perspective will become biased and narrow. Just remember, one of the qualities that's essential for stimulating intuitive muscles is variety.

Be creative in introducing your children to a love of adventure and discovery. The possibilities are unlimited because we live in a fascinating and fantastic universe. Finally, my teacher Dr. Tully always said that intuition works best when you have a strong foundation of knowledge. The more you know about people and the world, the more information you'll have to draw upon.

Creative Incentive

When you engage children's enthusiasm and give them an incentive, their sixth sense will kick in. My teacher Charlie Goodman taught me that this ability works a little differently for everyone. "Intuition follows our natural interest, which varies from person to person," he said. "Whatever we're drawn to, Divine awareness is right behind."

Twenty years ago, my husband, Patrick, had a friend named Phil who was living with his wife and their five-year-old son in a farmhouse in Iowa. It was Christmastime, and little Joey kept pestering his dad about his presents. Two days before Christmas, Phil finally said to him, "If you can find your gifts, then you can open them!"

This set Joey free. He looked high and low, but all he came up with were two very old boxes of Tide detergent that he found in the basement. One was open, the soap crusted over, but the other appeared to be intact. Phil threw the first box away and tossed the sealed one in the laundry basket.

The next day, the family went to the Laundromat to wash clothes. Phil opened the container of Tide, teasing Joey that this was his Christmas present. As he poured out the soap into the machine, a big wad of pre–Civil War silver certificates, stuck together in a solid brick, came tumbling out. Apparently someone had hidden them in the box and carefully resealed it.

All three stood with their mouths hanging open. What a find on Christmas Eve! The family quickly finished doing the laundry and raced home with their treasure. After thinking it over, they contacted an attorney for advice on what to do next.

Ultimately, a judge ruled that since they owned the house, the money was theirs free and clear! They sent the bills to the U.S. Treasury, which promptly returned a check for $35,515. Joey still talks about finding that box and says he's sure a Christmas angel showed him where to look.

Kids love to be intuitively challenged, especially if they have an incentive. Here's another example of how the sixth sense follows genuine interest and enthusiasm: Several years ago we lost our good Nikon camera. Patrick, the girls, and I looked everywhere, but after searching in every nook and cranny, we finally gave up. That evening at dinner, I suggested to Patrick that maybe it was for the best. Perhaps it was the Universe's way of telling us to retire the old thing. It was 15 years old, and even though my husband had a great affection for the camera that had accompanied him around the world, I'd secretly wanted to buy a new one for some time. Reluctantly, he agreed.

Sonia listened closely, and after a moment asked, "Dad, since you're getting another camera, if I find the old one, can I have it? After all, you won't need it anymore, right?"

"Sure, Wooze [my daughter's nickname]," Patrick answered.

"Would you teach me to use it?" she persisted.

"You bet. I'd be happy to."

For several days after that conversation, I overheard Sonia saying softly, "I wonder where that camera is."

One day as she was riding in the backseat of the car on the way home from school, she said, "I hope I find it, Mom. I really want it."

The very next day I had to go to the post office, and I took Sonia along with me. Annoyed at having to go, she flopped down in the backseat, pouting.

Just as I was shutting the car door, I heard Sonia ask, "What's this?" I turned around just as she was pulling a brown plastic bag out from under the seat on the driver's side.

I walked over to the curb and waited to see what she'd discovered. She sat up, opened the bag, and screamed. Then she threw the door open and yelled, "Mom, guess what? It's the camera! I found it!"

Sure enough, there it was, and it delighted her no end.

"Well, it's yours, Sonia," I said, very impressed. "Congratulations!"

She was beaming. By the time we got home, her father had arrived, too. "Dad, Dad, I found the Nikon!" she squealed.

Patrick was shocked, and he laughed out loud when Sonia told him the story. She kept repeating, "I *really* wanted that camera! That's why I spotted it." Then suddenly she sobered up. "Dad, don't worry. I'll let you borrow it anytime until you can afford one of your own."

"Thanks, Wooze," he said. "I appreciate that."

You can engage your kids' intuition very easily if you can discern where their real interests lie, but the key is discovering *their* passions—not yours. Joey's was Christmas presents, while Sonia's was a camera. What are your children's true interests? What do they care about?

Give Them a Vote

Yet another way to encourage your kids' intuitive growth is to give them a vote on what's happening in their lives. Wherever you can allow their input, do so. Whether it's decorating their room, dressing themselves, or deciding on extracurricular activities, let them choose what they like. Don't force them to silently acquiesce to your ideas of who they are, and don't put them in the position of having to make you look good. After all, it's *their* childhood, so let them enjoy it! Remember, whether it was good, bad, or otherwise, your own is over. You can recapture the child in you by playing with them, but don't squash *their* natural enthusiasm by taking all the fun out of it.

Let them make choices and express preferences, and allow them to have an opinion and speak without being censored. Of course, this doesn't imply anarchy—you should have family rules that establish respect, responsibility, and cooperation; but they don't have to suppress your children's individuality. In fact, you can invite them to participate in setting those expectations.

Also give them practice making decisions. After all, the point of enhancing our intuition is to make better choices. Of course, when there are questions of safety and protection, you must be in charge; but when you can let them decide on matters without endangering them, hand over the reins.

Invite their input on as many aspects of their life as is appropriate for their age. When they run to you for answers, first ask them how they'd solve the problem. When they express desires, have them come up with ideas about how *they* can fulfill them. And when they come to you to resolve a squabble they're having, request that they work it out among themselves. As much as is reasonable, encourage them to find their own way—you'll be surprised by what a little creative incentive can do for a kid's intuition.

Hanging a Bright-Idea Board

Another terrific way to nurture six-sensory living and creativity in your family is to create a "Bright-Idea Board," which is a bulletin board put up exclusively for the purpose of expressing and sharing great ideas. You can hang one in the kitchen, family room, or anywhere that everyone can have easy access to it.

Invite your spouse and children to write down all of their inspirations, insights, gut feelings, and suggestions as they arise and post them. For example, just this morning Patrick noted on our Bright-Idea Board: "It's dreary around here due to the gray weather, so let's have an international dinner tonight. Bring your favorite foreign dish." So this evening we're having a special meal, and I'm contributing an Indian treat called samosas.

And yesterday, Sabrina wrote to her sister: "Sonia, check your tires. I have a bad feeling about them." Sonia did have a look, and one of the tires was in dire need of air.

Establish creative sanctity around your board by insisting that everyone consider all the ideas that are contributed and not ridicule any of them. During family meetings, you can review and discuss the thoughts and suggestions that have been posted, as well as use them to fuel your brainstorms. It's fun, extremely productive, and encourages imaginative and intuitive thinking.

"I Just Gotta Be Me"

Another way to support children in developing the kind of creative expression that allows them to find and follow their own truth is to give them the freedom to choose their own style and taste in clothing. As any mother will admit, having a new baby to dress up can be a lot of fun. It's like having dolls all over again, only this time they're real!

It can be very easy to forget that our kids aren't playthings to be outfitted, molded, and forced to comply with our opinions of who they are. They're individuals with their own ideas and needs—as I was reminded quite pointedly by Sonia when she was three years old. . . .

One of my favorite pleasures in life is a *great* pair of shoes. I'm no Imelda Marcos, but I do appreciate good-looking styles and enjoy wearing them immensely. My affection for beautiful footwear spilled over into wanting it for Sonia and Sabrina as well. Many years ago when I worked for an airline, I frequently traveled to Europe, where I discovered that European baby shoes are simply the best in the world. I loved buying my daughters extremely "cool" brands that I could never find in the U.S. They had the snappiest, happiest feet this side of the Atlantic all through toddlerhood. The girls themselves were oblivious to their uptown appearance, but it was terrific fun for me.

One day I put Sonia in a magnificent pair of magenta and turquoise suede, high-top, lace-up boots that I'd bought in Italy—only to find her in the backyard 20 minutes later, slopping through mud puddles, the suede now destroyed.

"Sonia, come inside this minute!" I yelled at her from the kitchen window, upset that *my* new treasure had been wrecked.

She looked up at me, totally confused, and asked, "Why, Mommy?"

"Because you're ruining your boots!"

Annoyed, she stomped out of the puddle and came into the house.

"Ah, Sonia, just look at these shoes! They're shot," I lamented, peeling them off her feet.

"Mom," she answered, just as disgusted with me as I was with her, "next time please get them in *your* size! Okay?"

Her comment stopped me cold. She was so right that I had to laugh. It was true—I'd bought them for myself. I hadn't considered Sonia's personality for one second when I picked them out, but only my own. She wasn't a prima donna, but a rough-and-tumble, tree-climbing, trike-riding, sandbox-playing kind of girl. The boots were ridiculous for her. What she needed was a good pair of canvas sneakers or some rubber galoshes. All my projections of what I liked were cramping her style, and she let me know it in no uncertain terms. That was the last pair of European shoes I ever bought for Sonia.

Our conversation taught me a very important lesson in respecting who my children are: Choosing clothing, like all sensual activities, reveals their unique creativity. Ever since that episode, I've made a genuine effort to let my girls make their own wardrobe choices whenever practical. Almost invariably, both Sonia and Sabrina pick out something other than what I would have selected, and yet they always wear it to death. Giving them some autonomy supports their sense of individuality and is practical for our budget!

Kids need to be free to be creative, and that definitely includes letting them make decisions about how to dress themselves, as well as allowing them to play, get dirty, and *be a kid!* Recognize that choosing what to wear (with the obvious exception of items that may create problems, such as gang attire or shorts in a snowstorm) is part of their personal expression, and appreciate their sense of style.

A child's world is sacred and will help them connect with their Source. By the very fact that they can imagine, play, sing, paint, move, and laugh so easily, you know they're in touch with something Divine. Be fair: Don't intrude upon their free spirit or attempt to mold it, take it away, or live vicariously through it. Recognize their creativity as the language of the soul; and instead of suppressing it, brush up on this wonderful idiom and try relearning to speak it yourself. The next time your kids are coloring, dancing, inventing, singing, or dressing up, join them and get in on the fun!

Lighten Up

No matter what methods you use to engage your children's intuition, the most important thing is your attitude. If you're a perfectionist, control freak, or drama queen, then chances are that you'll have little success in creating an atmosphere of wonder and discovery, which is the necessary playground for young intuitives.

One of my own hobbies is collecting and studying the history of the tarot, which is based on pictorial books from the Middle Ages designed to teach mastery of life. In all tarot decks, the very first card is the Fool, a merry time traveler ready to descend to Earth to have a worldly experience. In his hand is a rose, symbolizing desire. On his back, he carries a satchel full of his talents. And at his feet is a little white dog, which represents his intellect, his soul's companion, and—above all—his light-footed spirit.

This card tells us to travel lightly. We all have to play the fool from time to time, and we need to laugh at our mistakes before we can learn from them. Doing so gives us perspective and sometimes insight. It also reminds us that who we are (spiritual beings and time travelers who are here on Earth to create) and what we do (make mistakes) aren't the same thing. It keeps our self-worth intact and emphasizes the need to look silly at times in order to gain wisdom.

If you laugh easily and are lighthearted, your children will feel safe and joyful about discovering life. Have you ever heard them giggling about nothing? About goofing up or being the fool? Left to their natural impulses, children laugh all the time. They only learn to stop doing so if no one else in the house joins in with them.

Be honest and easygoing enough to admit your errors to your kids. Tell them "I'm sorry," "I'm tired," "I need space," or "Give me a moment" when you need to. Be as democratic as possible as you do what's necessary to take care of yourself. Don't be a martyr, a boss, a victim, or a drag. Lighten up and play with your children! Intuition is a resonating energy, and whoever uses it sparks all the other family members to do the same.

Establishing New Habits

Have your children wonder:

- Who's calling when the phone rings
- Where you'll find a parking space
- When the elevator will come
- When the teacher will give a pop quiz
- Who will win the school football game
- What science project to do for an assignment
- Where their books or shoes are

Let a sense of adventure lead you to:

- Visit an unfamiliar part of town
- Attend a cultural arts performance
- Study another race
- Eat a type of food you've never tasted
- Travel to a different city or country
- Explore another religion
- Invite someone new to dinner

Give your kids a vote on:

- Who to be friends with
- What vegetable to eat for supper
- What to study in school
- How to spend your summer vacation
- Where to go for dinner

Allow your children to choose:

- What to wear
- How to decorate their rooms
- How to style their hair
- What music to listen to
- Their preferences, without insults or judgment

Together, try:

- Laughing
- Singing
- Telling jokes
- Trying new things
- Making mistakes without censure
- Being *very* curious
- Acting silly and playing the fool

Reflections

- Do you allow your own sense of awe to influence your life? How?

- Are you beginning to notice the subtle energy around you?

- Have you introduced the *I Wonder* game to your children? If so, what happened?

- Are you creating a sense of fun and delight when you play? When?

- What are some of the discoveries your wondering has led to?

- Where have you ventured with your kids lately?

- Are you encouraging them to flex their intuitive muscles? How?

- Is there any room for spontaneity in your family life? Give a few examples.

Reminders

Are you:

- Creating your own language of spirit?

- Remembering to clear your aura and your kids'?

- Being respectful of all vibes, however inconvenient or unpleasant they may be?

- Being playful and having adventures?

Recognizing your children's sense of wonder and their love for discovery and adventure is one of the keys in sparking their intuitive ability. Another essential element is art. In the next chapter, you'll be shown how all kinds of creative expression can help you and your family tune in to your Higher Selves.

Chapter Ten

ART OPENS THE HEART

A Direct Avenue to Intuition

All children begin life with direct access to their intuition and spirit. They tap into this realm through their creative play and spontaneous artistic invention, which is the domain of the soul. When they express themselves, whether through dance, music, drawing, storytelling, or some other form, they're actually sharing the contents of their inner world with us.

Unstructured playtime is the beginning of kids' six-sensory expression. They're highly aware and have many insights, but may not yet have a linear, structured language to verbalize them very well. Even so, youngsters can and do reveal their perceptions and feelings quite accurately all the time, through their drawing, singing, dancing, and music. It's up to us as parents to pay attention and recognize that their artistic expression is an important part of their souls, and a second—perhaps purer—medium they can use to communicate.

I've worked closely over the years with my intuitive friend Julia Cameron, who's a novelist, songwriter, and the author of *The Artist's Way* and many other books about creativity. She says that "artistic callings are God's marching orders to bring beauty and soul into the world." Furthermore, being connected to our heart and expressing ourselves puts us in a state of bliss. This explains why all kids so freely love to do art, for it's an instinctive way to tune in to their inner selves—that is, unless judgment and competition are introduced. When that occurs, the spirit exits and the ego takes over.

Encourage Enjoyment, Not Competition

I'm not suggesting that children don't need to learn the techniques of art. In fact, if they enjoy a creative pursuit, they'll love mastering the use of the materials. But when we emphasize technical skill more than the pleasure of personal expression and create a competitive atmosphere, a sensitive child's spirit may shut down and withdraw. For example, my friend Lu Ann told me that as a little girl, she loved playing the flute. Because it brought her so much joy, she practiced constantly. By the time she was in the third grade, she was quite proficient, joined the school band, and was put in the first chair.

In the beginning, she was thrilled by the honor, but soon she began to encounter hostility and sabotage from the other flute players. Suddenly, going to band practice actually became psychically painful for her. She was glared at in the hall, whispered about, shoved in the lunch line, and so harassed by the other flutists that she became very depressed.

Two months of this was all Lu could bear. She'd had enough of being "first," and simply wanted to play her beloved instrument.

One day during practice, she voluntarily stood up and deliberately walked back to the last chair and took a seat. Greatly relieved, she sat back and waited for the others. Everyone in the band was surprised and confused to find that she'd abandoned the coveted position. When Mr. Glutt, the band director, saw that she'd moved, he asked her why.

"Because I just want to play the flute," she answered. "In the first chair, it's too serious." And she stayed put. The other kids were surprised—some even acted embarrassed, and a few apologized. Mr. Glutt allowed her to stay in her chosen spot for the rest of the year.

Lu's story is more common than you may know. I'm often alarmed by the amount of competition, ignorance, and snobbery surrounding our children's artistic expression. Such ambitious attitudes can actually silence the important spiritual language our kids require to tap freely into the well of their souls. Art is the primary medium of the inner self, and they should never have to meet the standards of frustrated or ambitious parents, or vie with each other on tests. On the other hand, adults also must be careful not to dismiss creative expression as having no value by regarding it as "only play."

Art Gives the Soul a Voice

When parents express a denigrating attitude toward art, they influence their children to move away from their connection with their inner world. Kids feel this as an amputation on the soul level. Even worse, the severing of their spiritual ties allows intuitive disabilities to take hold and fester, often leading to depression and even addiction.

Many clients have come to see me for an intuitive consultation regarding their children's lack of focus or addictive behavior. In many such cases of general angst, I've noticed that their kids are suffering a serious loss of soul due to having been cut off from artistic expression. They're often the sons and daughters of well-intentioned, ambitious people who don't recognize the spiritual *value* of their children's creative interests, and consequently have discouraged them in favor of more "serious" studies or athletic activities.

However, these young people are so often the very souls who have come to Earth to help us all heal by giving us music, song, poetry, dance, sculpture, and all the other art forms that nurture our spirits. If they perceive at an early age that their soul purpose and expression has no value, they may then withdraw, shut down, and seek ways to stop their intuitive pain, often dulling their consciousness with drugs or food addictions.

The Soul Needs Art to Be Healthy

The best way to deepen your understanding of the value of art is to reconnect with it yourself. See it for what it is: the language of intuition and spirit. Can you imagine life without creative expression? Without color, sound, and sensuality?

Several years ago, Patrick, the girls, and I had a taste of such an existence; and it was eye-opening. We sold our house and purchased a new one that required a complete gutting and renovation. We then began looking for a temporary place to live during our project, which wasn't an easy task for a family of four and a dog.

We rejoiced when we found a small two-bedroom apartment in the neighborhood, which was very reluctantly rented to us on the condition that we didn't hang any pictures on the walls or change the "minimalist" decor in any way. We were so grateful to have a home at all that we didn't anticipate that the terms of the lease would create a hardship.

We put all our furniture into storage, including our art, music, and family photographs, and kept what we needed to get by. We tiptoed around our rented flat in a state of anxiety, looking at the empty beige walls and a tiny TV set.

Our painfully extended renovation went on for seven long months. During this period, we became increasingly depressed and irritable every time we walked in the door. Two of our babysitters quit, and the girls' schoolwork suffered. I thought I'd entered early menopause, and Patrick was on the warpath.

It wasn't obvious at first, but we eventually identified the source of our poor intuitive condition. Sonia said it best as we spent yet another evening surrounded by harsh lighting and bare walls: "Mom, we have to get out of here soon. This place just doesn't have any *flavor.*"

We couldn't have agreed more. In our overzealous desire not to offend the owners, we'd avoided creating any personal atmosphere whatsoever in the apartment, and we were now suffering terribly for it. Our spirits did indeed need flavor—the kind that comes from art, music, dance, and all the spontaneous, sensual expressions of the inner self. There was no doubt about it: Our souls were languishing.

The very day after we moved into our newly renovated house, we ripped through our boxes until we found what we were craving most. Our artwork was once again on the walls, one of Patrick's good soups was simmering on the stove, Sabrina's crayons and paints were spread all over the playroom floor, Sonia was banging on the keyboard, and my writing desk was standing proudly again. We *all* breathed a huge and grateful sigh of relief. In every sense of the word, we were once again *home*.

If you find yourself pushing your children's artistic development too hard, or if you're impatient with their creative efforts and want them to move on to more "serious" interests, ask yourself if perhaps you may have lost your own sacred connection to art. Maybe without consciously knowing it, you were cut off from your own soul food as a child, and now you're standing in the shadow of your kids' delight, wanting to taste it once again.

Know that neither living vicariously through your children's imagination nor casting darkness over it will help their spiritual awakening, nor will it heal your old wounds. I believe that artistic play and expression should be a family affair in which everyone participates, free from censorship, in an atmosphere of love and fun—no competition allowed.

Allow Art to Live in Your Home

I was fortunate to be raised in a family where creativity was nurtured and supported. My father was a gardener, carpenter, and painter; while my mother sewed, did photography, painted, and designed our home. And both of them *loved* to dance. Our home was in constant sensual motion, and we grew up around parties where the hi-fi blared and people enjoyed moving to the music. In fact, my brothers started a band, with two of them playing guitar and the other on drums. My three sisters sewed and designed their own clothing, and I danced.

Today, all seven of us are in creative professions. Two are interior designers, one creates furniture, and another is a computer graphics artist. In addition, I have one sibling who's a psychic healer, and I do intuitive readings. Above all, we're each comfortable with our sixth sense and have followed our hearts' desires all along. I believe that our connection to art kept us in touch with our inner selves and our true sense of the purpose of life.

My teacher Charlie Goodman put it beautifully: "Sonia, there are many ways to listen and hear the voice of your soul—through meditation, prayers, and even work at times. But if all else fails, connect with your spirit by using your hands. Be creative. The hands are linked to the heart, which is the seat of the soul. They'll always take you home."

Establishing New Habits

- Paint a picture.
- Write a fairy tale.
- Have fun with clay.
- Sing a song.
- Dance to your favorite music.
- Play the piano.
- Create a collage.
- Design an outfit.
- Invent a recipe.
- Make a mess.
- Do all the above with your children!

Reflections

- What are your favorite artistic interests or activities? What are your children's?

- Do you have a place in your house where you and your family can use your imagination and experiment?

- Do you or your kids set aside any time during the day to enjoy creative projects? When?

- Can you and your children pursue new modes of expression without having to be "good" at them?

- Have you had any intuitive insights while working on your art? What are they?

Reminders

Are you:

- Respecting all vibes, however inconvenient or unpleasant they may be?

- Being playful and having adventures?

- Taking time to express your personal art?

- Encouraging your family members to share their own creativity?

Chapter Eleven

ASKING FOR GUIDANCE

One of the most exciting things you and your children will discover when you actively call upon intuition is that you're infinitely supported in your goals. The Universe is ready, willing, and able to assist you; but before you can receive help, you must *ask* for it.

Requesting intuitive guidance is a habit your kids can learn from you. Let them know early on that they're sons and daughters of the Universe, which is watching over them and wants them to succeed in life. They respond well to the knowledge that the Divine is on their side and that they can tap into its support simply by asking.

When I tell kids that the Universe *wants* to assist them, their first question is, "What things can I ask for help with?" I answer, "Everything . . . except how to cheat." I explain that they're cared for so much that they're provided with love, protection, safety, inspiration, ideas, solutions, and all the other things they need to grow and thrive in life.

One child, Cheryl, asked me if the Universe would do her homework for her.

I replied, "No, it won't do it for you, but it will guide *you* to finish it."

"Rats!" Cheryl exclaimed, and then shrugged. "Oh well, at least it's something."

The world takes on a friendly, kind, and loving countenance for kids when they become aware that Divine energy is on their side.

And in an era when guns, violence, alcohol, and drugs are often just as much a part of their mental and physical landscape as dolls and baseball, it's very comforting for them to know that they have extra help available.

My mother introduced me to the practice of asking the Universe for help early on. Whenever I had a problem, whether it was finding my shoes or struggling because my best friend wasn't speaking to me, I learned to request guidance as soon as I realized I had a difficulty. One of the ways I did so was by playing a game my mom taught me called "fishing for solutions." I'd focus on my heart, cast my mind into the Universe like a fishing line, and ask it to catch an answer or idea for me.

I argued with her at first about whether it would actually work, but she insisted, "Sure it will, Sonia. Wherever there's a problem, there's always a solution. In fact, God gives us challenges just so we can enjoy the creativity and satisfaction of finding ways to resolve them. That's the fun of life!"

When I began "fishing," I'd wait only a moment or two before becoming impatient. "Mom!" I'd complain. "This is dumb. I'm *not* catching anything."

She'd respond, "Be patient, Sonia. This is no different from baiting a real fish. It takes time, and a solution won't come if you keep pulling on the line. Just relax and let your creative hook sit out there in the Universe for a while . . . and go do something else. When the idea comes, it will tug on your awareness and you can draw it in." So I'd try again. I'd cast my dilemma into the Divine "sea" and then forget about it.

I remember very clearly when I reeled in my first solution. I was having a lot of trouble with a new girl named Lillian, who'd just entered my third-grade class, lived in our neighborhood, and was extremely large and mean. For some reason, on her first day at our school, she decided that she hated me, but did like my two best friends, Sue and Vicky. In no time my pals had dropped me. I was deeply hurt by the rejection and betrayal, and for the first time in my life, I was frightened about my physical safety. Lillian often boasted about fighting, and I was afraid she'd actually beat me up.

I went to my mom for advice, and after a moment of reflection, she answered, "Hmm . . . I'm not sure what you should do, but I do have a suggestion. Why don't you ask your spirit to fish for a solution?"

I remember being annoyed with her idea because I felt as though she were using it as a way to dismiss me, but she stopped me in the middle of my complaint when I accused her of doing nothing.

"Sonia," she interrupted, "going to the Universe for help is *not* 'doing nothing.' It's the smartest possible choice because it opens your mind to new answers. Now go to your room and do your homework. Something will bite while you're studying—I'm sure of it!"

Not getting the instant satisfaction I wanted, I went off in a snit, but diving into my assignments calmed me down. I'm not exactly sure when I felt the first pull on the "solution line," but I was somewhere in the middle of my geography book when suddenly an idea popped into my mind.

It occurred to me out of "nowhere" that Lillian was an only child. Both Vicky and Sue were, too, and all three of them had parents who were separated and fathers who were rarely around. Maybe Lillian didn't like me because I had lots of brothers and sisters and a dad. Maybe she was jealous!

My fishing line tugged harder and told me to invite her to go swimming with my family at the Celebrity Lanes pool on Sunday night, which was our weekly ritual. It seemed like an odd idea, since Lillian hated me, but my intuition insisted.

I ran to my mother's sewing room and exclaimed, "Guess what, Mom? I think I caught a solution! Maybe I should ask Lillian to come swimming with us this weekend. What do you think?"

She thought for a moment and answered, "That's an interesting idea, Sonia. Why not? Give it a try."

When I called Lillian, she was surprised to receive an invitation from *me,* and there was a huge silence on the other end of the line. And then—to my great relief—she said, "Okay, but I have to ask my mom first. I'll call you back and tell you whether I can go when she gets home."

After dinner, Lillian phoned to say she'd be able to come, and she showed up on Sunday evening with her bathing suit. She jumped in the car with the seven of us kids and my dad (no seat belts in those days), and off we went. On the way over, she was so meek and mild that I didn't even recognize her, but at the pool, she warmed up and dropped her defenses.

We had a wonderful time. We jumped off the deep end, went down the slide, played shark, and laughed all the way home. She wasn't mean or angry at all, and from that night on, our battle was over. Soon we were playing with Vicky and Sue, who made up with me, and things settled back down to normal. I always attributed our friendship to the game my mother taught me.

You can teach your own kids to use the same technique whenever they're stuck. Simply suggest to them that their awareness is like a creative fishing line that they can drop into the unlimited sea of solutions and ideas anytime they need help. All they must do is focus on their heart, ask for guidance, cast their mind into the Universe, and wait for a nibble.

With very young children (and even those up to about six years old), you can actually use a toy or makeshift fishing line, which they love. With older kids, you can ask them to do the process mentally. Either way works, and it doesn't require anything more than the intention to reel in an idea and the receptivity to receive one. Solutions exist and are always available for those who seek them. As my psychic-development teacher, Charlie Goodman, once told me, where there's a problem, there's an answer, because they're attracted to each other like magnets.

When I taught my daughter Sonia to go fishing in the Universe at the age of six, she asked me, "What do we use for bait?" I replied, "Why, the trouble itself, of course. Solutions *love* to gobble up problems!" She seemed satisfied.

One thing I've noticed about rushed and hurried parents these days (myself included) is that rather than having the patience or taking the time to encourage children to find ways to solve their problems, we prefer to just hand them answers. After all, it's faster for us and may be very easy. However, it discourages creative thinking and takes away the potential joy they'll experience in discovering how to resolve challenges for themselves. Furthermore, we may give them advice that doesn't help them as we'd hoped.

My spiritual teachers *never* gave me solutions, only ways to find them on my own. Whenever I needed guidance, I had to *work* for it. For example, I'd often talk to Charlie about school and friendship. Never terribly popular, I often felt like an ugly duckling and was very self-conscious most of the time. I'd ask him why the girls in school didn't like me, or what I could do to change that, but he never answered me directly. Instead, he'd say, "That's a very good question, Sonia. Better ask Spirit for guidance on that one!"

As frustrating as it was, he did teach me to call on the Universe for help, which to my amazement would eventually arrive in the form of insights, inspiration, and "pops" of understanding. I discovered that my lack of popularity in school had everything to do with my interests. One time, my guidance told me, "You're simply a deep-sea diver in a crowd of water-skiers." That made me laugh and buoyed my spirits as I began to look for other "deep-sea divers."

Asking for Help

Because I grew up in a psychic household, fishing for solutions was only one way in which we received guidance. My mother also had an ongoing direct dialogue with Spirit, openly conversing with It as easily as she talked with us. It wasn't at all unusual for her to turn to her heart and ask—usually out loud—for the Universe to not only lead her, but to actually help her in every way to accomplish whatever she needed to do. If she required some assistance on one of her art projects, such as her painting, sewing, or photography, she'd summon Spirit to get on the job with her. She wasn't spacey or weird about it, but straightforward, simple, and to the point.

After taking a home-study course on photography for two years and graduating with honors, my mom wanted to open a studio in our basement. While setting it up, she spent more money than my dad wanted her to, and he got very cranky about it.

"I hope this hobby of yours doesn't continue to cost so much. We can't afford too much more!" he commented one day, making my mother quite angry.

"You're being insulting!" she retorted, extremely irritated about his lack of enthusiasm. "This is *not* a hobby, I'll have you know! I'm a professional! I'll pay for the studio with my own earnings, you'll see . . . *mark my words.*" (This was one of her favorite expressions.)

That night as I sat with her in the darkroom while she developed some photos she'd taken earlier of us kids, she took my hand and said, "Sonia, we need to call on the Universe to send me some work. Lots of it, in fact . . . and fast!" Then she turned to me and said, "Let's ask Spirit to bring me an abundance of projects and money so your father will calm down."

"Okay," I answered, as I stared at her closed eyes through the green glow of the darkroom light. "I'll ask, too, if you want." I quietly watched her pray for assistance. Then I closed my eyes and said to myself, "Divine Spirit, my mom needs lots and lots of work so Dad will stop complaining about the cost of her studio. Will you help her, please?"

After a moment, my mother squeezed my hand and told me, "Okay. I feel that Spirit heard us, and I'm sure It will get busy. Now let go. The Universe is on the job, so we can relax." It was as if the gentle pressure on my hand was a signal to trust and allow Spirit to do the work—so I did.

Less than a week later, I came home from school one afternoon with my brothers and sisters and found my mom rushing around, frantically straightening up the house. "Quick, help me clean up!" she told us. "We're having company any minute, and I want the place to look good!"

We dropped our books and began dashing around, plumping pillows and wielding the vacuum. "Who's coming?" I asked, gathering the morning newspaper off the couch.

She stopped and smiled. "You'll never believe it, Sonia!" she replied. "Your entire school—kids, teachers, and everyone—will be here soon, beginning with the principal."

"Why?" I asked incredulously. "What for?"

"Because I got a call today from Sister Mary Canisius asking me if I'd be interested in taking the school photos—from the first grade to the seniors, plus the teachers—starting this evening! It seems that the studio they normally use was overbooked this year and couldn't begin taking pictures for another two months. Sister Mary didn't want to wait, so she phoned to see if I was available instead! Can you believe it?"

"Wow, Mom! I guess the Universe really took us seriously when we prayed for *lots* of work the other night."

"It sure did . . . now let's get finished here," she said.

For the next two weeks, students filed through our front door and down to her basement studio, grade by grade. My mom did such a good job photographing each child that almost every parent ordered a picture. As a result, people began asking her to take family and company portraits, as well as wedding photos. Her business exploded overnight.

I was amazed by how generous and speedy the Universe had been in launching my mother's studio . . . and so was my father. All she'd had to do was ask—and, of course, *expect* to receive—and she was on her way.

Prayer

The most direct way to encourage your children to ask for help is to teach them to pray. Most kids like it once they learn how, and naturally do it in some form or another anyway.

My sister Cuky once told me a story about my nephew's early approach to prayer: She and her son Sean were walking hand in hand to the park one day when she was pregnant. Halfway there, Sean looked up at his mother's belly and told her, "Mom, there's just one thing I've *got* to know."

Expecting him to ask about the baby and how it got inside her, Cuky braced herself and replied, "Yes, what is it?"

He paused, thinking for another minute. "Well," he asked thoughtfully, "just what the heck is Mrs. God's name, anyway? I have to ask her for something, and I don't know what to call her!"

I've encountered very few people who pray in a productive way. I've observed that most don't release their requests into the heart of the Universe with any confidence that they'll receive help. Instead, they continue to hold on to their worries with a vicelike grip.

In fact, the key to success in this area is learning to turn your problem over to God. Once you've asked for support, don't keep dwelling on your concerns. Whenever my mom prayed with us, she always ended with a squeeze of her hand and a message to let it go: "It's done. Now let's relax!" By doing so, she infused our prayers with faith. The gesture seemed to be the indefinable something that transformed our requests from wishful thinking and fearful whining into a powerful and profound sense of conviction. When she squeezed our hands, the Universe was on the job!

You can pray with your children any way you like. You can do it formally; in the morning or at night; and on your knees, at the table, or in bed. Alternatively, you can share what I learned: to live in a state of constant prayer and ask for help whenever the need arises. The best way to teach your children to do this is to have them watch you call on the Universe for guidance—or better yet, do so together. After all, example is the most effective teacher.

My friend Wendy's grandfather was a faith healer and prayed aloud all the time. She says she remembers that on many occasions when she and her four siblings were riding in the car with him and indulging in their usual squabbles, he'd burst out: "Dear God, we pray to Thee to *heal* all the temperamentalness of someone in this automobile! We won't say who it is, so as *not* to embarrass anyone, but he or she *knows* who they are. Amen."

Laughing, Wendy recalled, "Every time Grandpa did this, we'd all get very quiet. After all, we didn't know what 'temperamentalness' meant, but it didn't sound very good. Besides, we didn't want to humiliate ourselves by being the guilty one!

"Corny or not, his prayer always worked," she continued. "And because it was so effective for him, I've used it myself to this day, particularly when I'm around someone who's causing trouble. It works as well for me as it did for him—especially if I say it out loud," she said, smiling.

My mother's style was to pray anytime and anywhere, asking for whatever a situation required—from help finding her keys to sending healing energy to a sick friend. All that was needed was a bowed head, closed eyes, and inward reflection. Sometimes she prayed out loud, and other times she did it silently.

My friend Suzanne's mom was also a "pray-er," but she was more formal, preferring to kneel down and say rosaries in the morning. Lu Ann's mother created a sacred atmosphere first, enlisting the aid of holy water, incense, and candles. And yet another friend's mom played religious music (usually Gregorian chants).

Whatever approach you take, the truth is that it's your choice. After all, prayer is really a private chat with God, and any method is valid if you're sincere. Whether you prefer a more spontaneous or ritualized style depends upon your own needs.

Gratitude as Prayer

One of the most powerful ways to pray is to practice gratitude, which clears the lens of your consciousness like windshield wipers in a storm. It brushes off the confusion and helps you see the world more clearly.

Practicing gratitude is very easy and immediately rewarding. All you need to do is acknowledge and thank the Universe for your blessings, whether they include good health, family, friends, or simply being alive. I keep a personal gratitude journal; and as a family, we use our kitchen bulletin board to post photos of happy experiences and note our appreciation for the things we've received. It's amazing to realize just how much we all have to be grateful for once we begin to notice.

Stopping to recognize the many gifts we've been given instantly lightens our spirits and helps us remember how much we're loved and supported by the Universe. Whenever my daughters and I are restless, irritable, anxious, bored, or uneasy, I suggest that we think of as many things as possible to be thankful for in order to change our energy. We list our blessings one at a time, trying to come up with at least ten. Every time we do this, our fear subsides, and our hearts and intuition open.

Practicing gratitude keeps children's awareness focused on the abundance, support, and love that the Universe has for them. It directs their hearts and attention to receiving all that's available to them, and reminds them to remain in a state of receptivity and peace.

I've described only a few ways to ask for Divine guidance, and you may have an entirely different one. Some people chant or sing their prayers, while others say them silently or use beads or rosaries. Still others pray in groups, have an ongoing dialogue with God, or meditate. All methods and traditions are valid.

Your prayer style is very personal, so use whatever approach you prefer. Know that God loves you completely and unconditionally as you are, faults and all. Whether you're calling on Spirit by yourself or with your kids, realize that the Universe *wants* to help, but first you must ask.

The master teacher Jesus Christ underscored the importance of prayer when he was questioned about miracles. "Of myself, I do nothing," he said. "It is my Father in Heaven that works through me." In the Bible, it also says: "If God is for us, who can be against us?" The truth is that there's no greater power than God.

Establishing New Habits

— **Fishing for solutions.** As a family, get into the habit of seeking guidance together. Whenever someone has a quandary, dilemma, problem, or issue, invite everyone to cast their creative lines into the Universe and reel in support, inspiration, answers, and direction to help that person. Pull in everything that comes up, and don't censor anything. If an idea doesn't work, you can always throw it back. The more your family collaborates on this technique, the more delightful and creative the outcome will be.

— **Pray together.** The most powerful prayers are those you send with the full awareness that you're a beloved child of God. When you ask for Divine guidance from a place of deep knowing that the Universe wants to support you, delight you, and love you unconditionally, your requests are more quickly satisfied. When you pray with others who share your faith, it works even better.

Designate a time when your family can call on Spirit together. This can be at dinner, before bed, or after your weekly meeting. It's also important to encourage individual members to ask the others to pray with or for them whenever they're feeling upset or concerned or need a little extra support.

As Jesus said: "When two or three are gathered in my name, there I am with them."

Asking with Art

One of the most delightful ways to integrate art with asking the Universe for support was shown to me by Lu Ann Glatzmaier, who has been my friend since I was 14 years old. I was introduced to her by my mother, to whom she'd come for lessons on how to do psychic readings. Our paths have been parallel from the beginning: Both of us showed unusual intuitive abilities at an early age, and we've both become healers.

Lu taught me to make what she called an "alchemy box." Over the course of several sessions, we each decorated a box inside and out with tissue paper, stickers, affirmations, spiritual emblems, and images of angels.

When they were completed, we placed all of our special written requests and prayers inside as a symbolic act of surrendering them in faith so that the Universe could work on them. To my amazement and delight, every time I put a note in my box, it was eventually answered.

Other names for these hand-decorated containers are *wish box, prayer box, angel box,* and even *911 miracle box!* I refer to them as alchemy boxes because *alchemy* means transmutation or change.

Whatever you call it, making something beautiful to hold your prayers brings out the child in everyone. It was the activity of choice for both Sonia and Sabrina at their birthday parties because, as they'd say, "Even though we already have alchemy boxes, we want our friends to have them, too. Every kid needs one!"

My daughter Sonia used lots of stickers and magazine photos of animals and fish because she's crazy about them. She put blue tissue paper on the inside, as well as stickers of dolphins and other sea creatures; and she covered the outside with brown and green tissue paper and pictures of horses, lions, cats, dogs, and elephants.

The themes for Sabrina's box were more mythical and celestial: She wrapped the exterior in blue tissue paper and images of moons, stars, suns, angels, saints, rainbows, and comets; and she decorated the interior with hearts.

Making these treasures was a family affair, and we spent weeks preparing our materials. We chose boxes from our closets, bought tissue paper, pored over past issues of *National Geographic,* and cut out pictures. We went to the stationery store for stickers, and visited an arts-and-crafts shop for acrylic coating, sprinkles, and glue. The process was fun and created a sense of anticipation.

The day finally came when we all sat down at the kitchen table and began to assemble our boxes, talking all the while about the elements we especially loved. We discussed the decorations we chose to use and why. When we were finished, we sprayed them with clear acrylic to protect them. We laughed and had a delightfully creative day preparing a place to keep our requests safe while the Universe worked on them.

When the boxes were complete, we each put a prayer inside. Then Patrick, Sabrina, Sonia, and I held hands and asked Spirit to send us guidance and bless our miracle boxes and all of us.

Over the years, we've developed an annual ritual: On New Year's Eve, we pull out our boxes and put our wishes and prayers for the upcoming year inside. Then on New Year's Day, we open them again and read our list from the year before. Every time we do this, we laugh and cheer at how many special requests were answered.

Making an alchemy box really captures children's imagination and teaches them, through creativity, art, and invention, how to surrender prayers to the Universe. Once they've created a box, you can suggest that they write any special requests or spiritual emergencies they may have on a piece of paper and put them inside—at any time, for any reason. The very act of doing this helps kids focus on their needs, actually *ask* for Divine help, and then release their requests with faith. It also teaches them to be patient, let go of their worries, and *allow* the Universe to work on their behalf.

An alchemy box combines creativity with an open heart and a receptive mind. It establishes a way of thinking that connects them to their Source. The combination of art and prayer helps them access all the love, guidance, and protection of the Universe, using their own imagination and creativity. When we feel alone, life is tough. It's so much easier for your kids when they know they have God's infinite power on their side.

Making Your Own Alchemy Box

Supply list:

> *Shoe box*
> *Colored tissue paper*
> *Glue stick*
> *Stickers of inspiring images*
> *Glitter*
> *Holy cards*
> *Affirmations*
> *Photos*
> *Pictures of your heart's desires*
> *Acrylic coating*

Gather your supplies over a period of several weeks and plan a time to decorate your box. As you work, play inspirational and uplifting music.

This is also a wonderful activity for a children's party. In fact, everyone, young and old, needs an alchemy box for special requests. Make the time to create one, and let it begin to work for you.

Reflections

- Have you taught your children how to fish for solutions? Have they tried? When?

- Are they getting results?

- Have you "fished" as a family? Did you catch anything interesting?

- Do you pray? If so, when? Do you do so with your children? When?

- Do you ask each other for help in calling for Divine guidance for special intentions?

- Do your kids make requests to the Universe on their own? How?

Reminders

Are you:

- Being playful and having adventures?

- Using your artistic talents?

- Remembering to ask for guidance?

- Aware that the Universe loves you and wants to help?

As you've seen, there are many ways to connect to the Universe and ask for its help. In the following chapter, you'll learn more about the angels, guides, and other helpers who answer your calls for assistance.

Chapter Twelve

ANGELS, HELPERS, AND GUIDES

Growing up in an intuitive household really instilled an added sense of confidence in me that I'm grateful to be able to pass along to children. It isn't a strength that arises from an egotistical feeling of "I can do it by myself." Rather, it's the sense of relief that comes from knowing that I *don't* have to accomplish everything on my own. I only have to do my part, and the Universe will meet me halfway with support, protection, and guidance.

The inner assurance my mother imparted to me took on an even more wonderful dimension when I began my intuitive apprenticeship with my teacher Charlie Goodman when I was 12 years old. One of the first things he taught me was that God loves each and every one of us so much that the Universe actually provides us with our own "staff"—a group of spirit guides whose sole purpose is to assist, support, direct, protect, instruct, and delight us as we work to fulfill our purpose in life. Almost every child has many encounters with their loving guides, whereas we adults have just learned to ignore them.

One of my clients, Robin, told me about encountering her spirit guides when she was a kid:

"When I was a little girl, I distinctly remember seeing two spirit guides in my house. They were both from India and were dressed all in white, kneeling in the hallway with their heads bowed and their hands clasped in prayer. When I saw them, they lifted their heads as if to say they were watching over me, then resumed their prayerful position. I wasn't sleeping or dreaming, and I wasn't sick or hallucinating. It was daytime, and I was perfectly conscious and completely awake!"

Her eyes were wide as she recounted her story, "After I saw them, I told my mother, and surprisingly enough, she believed me, even though it spooked her a little! Sonia, what do you think I saw?"

Of course I thought she'd seen her spirit guides, and I told her so. Then I asked her, "How did the experience make you feel?"

"Well, after the initial shock, I felt happy and safe . . . as though I had two extra sets of eyes watching out for me. I liked the feeling of their presence, because it gave me a sense of companionship. I thought about them often—so much so that I learned to meditate when I was a teenager. I've even studied the Hindu religion in some depth. It has helped keep me from being a nervous wreck in life, especially when I was a wallflower in high school!"

Yes, they were guides for sure!

Your Spiritual Staff

We all have spirit guides who help us with our day-to-day activities; as well as with our physical, emotional, and spiritual development. Their only purpose is to make our lives easier, more enjoyable, and full of wonder. There are several different types of guides, each with their own specialty; and all of us have a "staff" of these marvelous light beings assigned specifically to us.

Runners

We all have guides called "runners" to help us find things. They're there for us when we can't locate our shoes, our keys, our school books, a parking space, a seat at the movie theater during the first week's release of a hit film, or anything else we're looking for. Children love having runners because they're forever losing their belongings.

My client Francine called me to tell me how much easier her life has been ever since she introduced the notion of a runner spirit guide to her son, Max, who's four years old.

"Before we knew about runners, Max was constantly losing things, and I'd spend hours of my day searching for them," she told me. "Whether it was his coat at school, his shoes at a friend's house, or his favorite stuffed monkey just before bed, a day never went by that we didn't have a big upset and drama over his lost stuff.

"Then one day, after learning about spirit guides, I told Max that he had a very special assistant who'd help him find everything he misplaced.

"He was intrigued and asked, 'Really? My own guide? What's his name?'

"'You tell me, Max,' I answered. 'After all, he's *your* guide.'

"'Mmm . . . Chester! That's his name!' Max announced without hesitation.

"'Great!' I said. 'Now let's put Chester to work, starting with asking him to find your missing sneaker, the one we've been looking for for weeks.'

"Max closed his eyes and said, 'Chester, take me to my shoe.' And off they went. He raced from room to room on a wild hunt, giggling all the way. After a 15-minute search, I heard him squeal with delight, 'Mom, we found it!' And he came running into the kitchen with the truant shoe dangling from his fingers. Breathless and triumphant, he exclaimed, 'Chester's real! He told me to look in my desk drawer, and there it was! We got it!'

"He was so thrilled with his find that he's been asking for Chester's help ever since. He still loses things all the time, but with Chester on the job, it's never a battle to get him to search for them. In fact, it's fun!" Francine said, smiling.

Helpers

We also each have another spirit guide called a helper, who shows up to help us with projects. Because our tasks change, so do our helpers. Older kids of nine years of age and up especially appreciate these guides because this is the time in their school lives when they're beginning to be asked to do more independent work. June, another client, told me this story about her 11-year-old daughter Marcy's encounter with a helper:

Never the studious type, Marcy was completely demoralized when she was given an assignment in class to write about the farming industry in France, a topic she had absolutely no interest in and even less desire to investigate. After watching her mope around and put it off for several days, June finally suggested to Marcy that she ask her helper guide for assistance.

"What can a guide do?" Marcy complained. "I still have to write the paper!"

"I don't know," June answered. "Ask and see."

So Marcy said, "If I have a helper, will you please *help* me!" and left it at that.

Later that afternoon, June asked her daughter if she wanted to ride with her out to the airport after school the next day to pick up a visiting friend.

"Sure," Marcy said, relieved that her mother wasn't going to insist that she stay home and work on her project.

A short while into the drive, Marcy switched on the radio and began turning the dial, looking for something interesting to listen to. As she searched the airwaves, she heard a French accent and stopped. She'd tuned in to a program on National Public Radio, and just by chance, an interviewer was talking to a group of nuns from a monastery in central France who completely supported themselves by running their own farm. The discussion was fascinating, and because Marcy had just come from school and was carrying her books, she was prepared to take notes. At the end of the show, the announcer gave instructions on how to order a transcript of the interview, which Marcy also scribbled down.

Her formerly dry topic now animated with real people and their personal stories, Marcy was completely engaged. She wrote a beautiful essay on the nuns' experience and got an A+ for her efforts. After her paper was returned, Marcy remarked to her mom, "It was lucky that I happened to turn on the radio at that moment and hear the program, don't you think? Do you suppose maybe it was my guide coming to my rescue?"

"Of course," June replied with a smile. "And what a good job your helper did!"

Teachers

In addition to runners and helpers, we also have spirit teachers who oversee our spiritual awakening. I believe that these were the guides Robin saw as a child. And when I was little, I had many, many recurring dreams of being in France and watching a stream of priests circle around me, praying for me. The dreams were fascinating, compelling, and very comforting. Subsequently, I've spent a great deal of time studying French and religion—especially medieval Catholicism and its connection to mysticism and spirituality. I'm sure that what I saw in my sleep was a team of visiting spirit teachers directing my path in this life.

Healers

We're also given spirit guides called healers, who help us stay healthy, balanced, and full of vitality. This is who whispers, "Time to go to sleep now!" or "Better not eat one more piece of candy!" A spirit healer is also the one who will come to children in their dreams and say, "I love you . . . you're safe," when their parents are divorcing and they're afraid and full of despair.

Healers comfort, counsel, and support our well-being. My client Denise called me one day and told me the following story about her five-year-old son Brian's encounter with a healer.

Brian had developed pneumonia and was suffering from a serious fever and deep-seated cough. He was delirious with pain and was flopping all over his bed in great discomfort for hours. Denise was beside herself with distress and anxiety over her inability to calm him down. Overwhelmed, she cried out into the night, "Healers, help me! Please!"

Several minutes later, Brian's entire body started to relax, and he seemed to have become focused on something in his mind's eye. "Mommy, see the beautiful lady over there?" he asked, transfixed with wonder by whatever he was looking at.

Denise began to get the shivers, and she replied, "No, honey, I don't. Tell me about her."

Brian didn't answer, and his eyes seemed to be following the woman. Apparently she was coming closer. He laid his head back, closed his eyes, smiled serenely, and said, "That feels good!"

He lay quietly for a few more minutes, breathing easily and deeply for the first time in days. Slowly, he opened his eyes, which were now sparkling, and waved good-bye, continuing to smile. Then he shut his eyes again and fell into a deep, contented sleep till morning.

"I'll never know who or what he saw that night," Denise told me. "All I'm certain of is that within five minutes of my plea for help, Brian saw something that calmed him for the rest of the night. Some might say it was only a fever-induced hallucination. Maybe so, but I believe the Universe answered my prayer, and I'm very grateful."

Joy Guides

We all have joy guides, who actually show up in groups! They're the ones who visit us when we need a dose of lightness, silliness, and pleasure. I'm sure you've experienced them. For example, have you ever heard a bunch of children giggling wildly, just for the sake of it? And the more they laughed, the more they cracked themselves up. Cutting up, clowning around, and being nonsensical are joy guides' delight. They appear at sleepovers, on school buses, and sometimes during movies. They especially like to stop by when you're lecturing your child and looking fairly ridiculous yourself. They tease, tickle, and—above all—restore perspective. They visit often and leave their healing touch on all who are around. Consider yourself lucky when joy guides come calling. It's a gift!

Angels

All guides are benevolent spiritual forces who lovingly come to aid us and our children with the sole purpose of restoring balance, providing direction, giving inspiration, and making us laugh. We can tell when we've been visited by one because we'll always feel somehow reassured. Angels are guides who protect us, and keep us on our path and out of danger so that we can fulfill our life's purpose.

Children also have angels who watch over them; and many, many kids have had wonderful encounters with them. My friend Karen told me a delightful story about meeting an angel when she was a teenager. She said that when she'd first learned to drive at the age of 16, she often tooled around her hometown of Baltimore in an old hand-me-down family jalopy. She'd push the fuel gauge to the limit because, like many young people, she had a car, but little money to keep gas in it.

Late one foggy night as she was coming home from a friend's house, the vehicle sputtered to a stop on an expressway running through what she called "a really crummy neighborhood." The tank was empty, and she started to pray because she was scared to death and didn't want to set out on foot.

Help me, God! she cried to herself. *I'm in trouble.*

Ten seconds later, an ancient beat-up car pulled up behind her, and out jumped an old Asian man with a gas can in his hand. With a nod and a smile, he opened the fuel cap, poured in the gas, and then put the cap back on. With another nod and a salute, he left without saying a word. As he drove away, Karen noticed a bumper sticker on his rattletrap that read: "Praise the Lord."

"He came out of nowhere, as though he weren't even real," my friend told me. "In fact, I'm sure he was otherwordly. After he left, I turned the key, and my engine started up right away. I was so relieved that I cried all the way home!"

Kids—especially very young ones—often talk to their guides and angels. When they play quietly, you may even hear them having very animated discussions with their spirit helpers; and if you ask, your children may tell you their names. Adults usually dismiss these interactions as just a game, and yet the way to the intuitive heart is through the openness and playfulness of a child.

Let me share an interesting experience my family had with my daughter Sabrina's angel: One day several years ago, Patrick, the girls, and I were in Iowa celebrating the 40th birthday of Patrick's brother Gene. We'd gathered together with about 30 family members and friends on an old farm in the country for a barbecue. It was October, and with nightfall approaching, a chill had set in. A huge campfire was lit, and everyone sat around it and began telling stories.

I was on one side of the crackling blaze with Sabrina and Sonia (then four and five years old), while Patrick was across from us. After a while, he pulled a bag out of the cooler and said, "Let's roast marshmallows."

Sabrina instantly shot up from her seat and raced over to her dad to get to the bag first. As she ran, she lost her balance and began to fall directly into the flames. Everyone screamed, and horror overwhelmed me as I realized that I was too far away to grab her.

All of a sudden, defying gravity, her body leaned away from the fire and spun around as though she'd been pushed. She fell to the ground as everyone gasped. Patrick and I rushed to her. "Sabrina!" I cried. "My God, are you all right?"

"I'm fine! That guy saved me!"

"What guy?" I asked.

"The one who pushed me away," she answered, puzzled. "There he is, see?" Sabrina pointed to the space behind the crowd, but we saw only the darkness of night. Everyone was a bit startled, but I understood and started to cry. She was pointing to her angel.

Later that night, as I put her to bed, she was just getting ready to fall asleep when she bolted upright, her eyes wide open. "Look at the sparkles!" she exclaimed, staring into the corner. Her eyes darted about, full of delight. "See them?"

I turned to look but saw only the darkened room. She sat fascinated for a minute, then said, "It's over. Did you see them?" as she beamed from ear to ear. I hadn't, but I knew that the angels were working overtime that night!

My friend Sarah's daughter, Anna, who is three years old and very fascinated with angels, is especially comforted by the idea that they keep her safe. Sarah told me a story about how her little girl began to find her courage when she knew that she had an angel by her side.

Anna was attending a summer day camp in the mornings, and after initially being anxious, found herself really looking forward to going—until one day, when she was told that the following morning, her group was going on a field trip. Anna never responded well to her routine being disturbed, and not surprisingly, she reacted negatively to the idea right away.

"Mommy, I don't want to go to camp today," she said to Sarah as they buckled their seat belts.

Sarah, a highly intuitive mother who was sensitive to her daughter's feelings, knew she was nervous about the outing. Recognizing this fear of change and new things, and sensing that the trip itself wouldn't be a problem, Sarah replied, "But Anna, today's your field trip."

"That's *why* I don't want to go. I'm scared!"

Sarah thought for a moment about how to reassure her and help her overcome her worry, and then remembered her daughter's fascination with angels.

"Well, Anna, if you're afraid, how about if we ask your angels to go with you and keep you safe?"

"Hmm . . ." the girl murmured, thinking it over.

"I'll go first, okay?" said her mom. "Angels, please surround Anna and protect her while she goes on her trip today." Then she turned to her daughter and told her, "Now it's your turn."

Anna thought for a moment longer, and then prayed, "Angels, watch over me and keep me and Mommy safe. The end." Then she smiled.

"Okay, Anna, now that the angels are on the job, how do feel about going on the field trip?"

Satisfied with her request for angelic accompaniment, she answered, "I'm all right now. I want to go." And she went from being afraid to running eagerly through the front door of the day camp without a moment's hesitation.

The notion of spirit guides may seem a little far-out or may not agree with your spiritual beliefs. Perhaps you've been introduced to guides in a different way. Catholics call on saints and angels for help; and in other faiths, people ask the souls of their ancestors to watch over and guide their families. Still others believe in spirits of nature—including the sun, the moon, and the wind.

Whatever tradition you draw from is the right one for you. The important thing to remember about spirit help is that we aren't isolated on our life's journey. Each one of us is part of the Universe and the heart of Divine Spirit. We're loved and protected. In fact, the entirety of creation conspires for our successful life's journey, and it's simply up to us to open our hearts and accept the loving hand of assistance.

The world can be a scary place, and kids of all ages are very conscious of the atmosphere of caution and suspicion that exists in these crazy times. But what starts as a healthy fear of strangers can sometimes become so big that it erodes a child's confidence. By adding spirit guides to the equation, you can reassure kids that there are greater forces out there who love them, watch over them, and keep them safe every day. And when children have the protection of their guides, they begin to relax.

Establishing New Habits

- Get to your spiritual staff—they lovingly seek to serve you.

- Talk with your children about their guides and your own.

- Give your spirit guides names and ask them to help you daily. In addition, talk about how they *do* support you.

- Thank them for their assistance out loud and often, and encourage your kids to do the same.

Reflections

- Have you or your children ever sent your runners on a mission or asked a healer to help you? Describe what happened.

- Have you ever had joy guides visit your family? When?

- Have you or your kids ever had an experience with an angel? Explain what it was like.

- How do you and your children feel about having guides?

Reminders

Are you:

- Being playful and having adventures?
- Using your artistic talents?
- Remembering to ask for help?
- Getting to know your guides?

Your guides are always available to help you and make your life more enjoyable, and hearing their messages requires a quiet mind. In the next chapter, we'll explore some fun and simple ways that you and your children can calm your thoughts and emotions and connect to Spirit.

Chapter Thirteen

QUIET TIME

As I mentioned in Chapter 1, even though asking for spiritual guidance is one part of awakening intuition, quieting our mind enough to hear it is the other. We have to tune in so that we can pick up the broadcast of Spirit. Although it may take an effort on the part of hurried and pressured adults to make time for inward reflection, children naturally fall into such contemplative states—if only parents will notice. It might occur when they're building with blocks, playing on a swing set, or digging in the dirt. They also may daydream in the car or stare into space at the dinner table.

My client Linda called me to tell me about her nephew Paul, who'd just visited her for the weekend. She told me that she lived in a high-rise building with a rooftop pool, and she decided that going there would be a fun thing for them to do together. When they arrived, Linda said to Paul, "You go ahead and swim. I'm just going to sit by the side and read for a while. Let me know when you're ready to go."

Paul jumped into the water, and Linda settled in with her book. After some time had passed, she suddenly noticed that it was very quiet. She looked over to the pool and saw Paul floating on a raft with his eyes half closed, staring into the water as if in a trance. Surprised to find him in such a tranquil state, she watched him for a while. He lay there motionless for another ten full minutes, and then slowly he blinked, stretched, looked over at her, and smiled.

"Paul, what were you doing?" Linda asked.

Calmly, he answered, "Oh, just meditating."

Linda was surprised, to say the least. She could hardly imagine that anyone in Paul's family, including her sister, would be interested in such activities.

"Meditating? Who told you about that?" she asked.

"I'm not sure," Paul replied. "I just know about it. I do it all the time and get good ideas!"

Whatever method they use, notice how your kids find a way to simply "zone out" and turn inward when they need to, even if it's only for a moment or two. This behavior is a natural meditation that relaxes the mind and thoughts, and tunes them in to the voice of the soul. Respect their daydreaming and let them have their reveries. When they come out of their quiet periods, you can ask them how they feel. You can also let them know that what they're doing is called meditation and that it's a good way to hear intuition.

Travel is so important to our children, but it does involve a great deal of stress because everything is new, different, and often out of our control. For Sonia and Sabrina, it means leaving the comfort of home, familiar surroundings and routines, and the company of their friends—which isn't easy for them.

One day a few years ago, we were driving in the rain, heading toward home after an extended trip. Sabrina said quite spontaneously, "You know, Dad, when I have to spend the night in places I've never been before, instead of getting scared, I just think of my favorite toy and everything I like about it for as long as I can. Then I relax and feel like I'm in my own bed, and I fall asleep."

"Sabrina, what a good idea!" I responded, very impressed. "The name for that is *meditating.*"

"Maybe, but I like calling it 'dreaming of my favorite toy' instead. It sounds nicer to me and helps me feel better." And then she continued to stare out the window, slipping back into her own private thoughts.

This reminded me of how children naturally do the right thing and how we need to notice that. Sabrina's method was a great suggestion for teaching other kids how to tune inward.

I really believe that there are many ways to achieve a state of inner tranquility and that sitting quietly is only one method.

Sabrina focuses on something she loves, Paul floats in the pool, Sonia daydreams as she listens to soft classical music, and her friend Madelyn calms herself by playing the piano. And believe it or not, some kids are best able to turn inward when they're in motion. I call this *active awareness,* and it's an equally valid way to connect to one's soul. For energetic children, this approach to quieting their emotions and thoughts is often a lot more practical.

Listening in Motion

One day my client Diane came to me for a reading because she was quite concerned about what she called my "nine-year-old banshee"—her very hyperactive, athletic son, Lonnie, who never gave her a moment's peace. I could tell that he was indeed wearing her out with his inability to be calm and quiet, and she was at her wit's end.

"I have him in every sort of sport, Sonia," she told me. "We live in a great neighborhood where he can play outside. We try to do things together as a family, but he's always so worked up and hyper that it's driving me mad. I can't seem to get him to settle down, and he's hard to be around. He's on Adderall, and it helps, but not much. Any ideas?"

I could tell from his intuitive makeup that he was indeed a very agitated kid with a lot of energy, and he was extremely frustrated about not being able to calm himself. My guides offered me one suggestion, so I passed it along to Diane.

"Get him interested in growing and caring for a garden," I advised.

"What?" she asked.

"See if you can involve him in working in a garden," I repeated. "My guides say that he's too fiery and that he needs more earth to quiet his nervous system."

"That's an interesting idea. Do you think he'll want to?"

"I don't know, but give it a try! Tell him that you need his help to get one going, and let him choose what to grow."

Diane left willing to attempt it. Six months later, she called me back. "Your suggestion was terrific!" she exclaimed. "Lonnie's out there with me all the time, taking care of his garden. He loves the earth and has his hands in it every day, generally for half an hour or so. We've grown tomatoes, lettuce, and radishes; and now he's into flowers. He takes great pride in his achievement. Since he's begun working there, his temperament has mellowed out big-time."

Even though he's still active in baseball and soccer, Lonnie's time in nature taught him to become calm and connect with his spirit. Using his hands, quieting his mind, and focusing only on gardening for a short time every day was a wonderful "kid meditation" for him.

Creative Visualization Techniques

Another great way to help your children focus inward and tune in to their inner selves is through a technique called creative visualization, which is basically giving them positive suggestions through imagery. Because most kids have such active imaginations and are so responsive to their parents, this is a highly powerful tool for their meditative lives.

Have them relax and get comfortable, preferably even lying down with their eyes closed. Once they're ready, you can very quietly and steadily guide them through a visualization that will calm them even more, as well as give them supportive messages to enhance their self-esteem and help them feel good about themselves.

I practiced a visualization routine with both my daughters when they were young that we called our "inner journey." Every night after they had their baths, read a book, and were ready for bed, I had them shut their eyes and listen to my voice while I told them how wonderful their spirits were and that they should think of everything they were proud of. I asked them to remember their victories, forgive their anger, let go of their frustration, visualize improving the areas they wanted to be better, and then peacefully go to sleep, knowing that God, their angels, their guides, and all of their family members and ancestors loved them completely.

I varied the "poem" or what I said to them from night to night, but always gave each of them a five- or six-minute visualization about feeling good about themselves just before going to sleep. It was a form of healing that we shared and was very grounding for all of us.

Anyone can do this with children—all it takes is a relaxed state, no interruptions, an easy tone of voice, and a heartfelt flow of loving images that are intended to calm and soothe. In order to be so tranquil, however, you may need to do a little preparation. For example, it's best to do the "inner journey" visualization after your kids have already begun to unwind a little. You can begin the process by having them take an aromatherapy bath just before bed, adding the essential oils of chamomile and lavender to the water. Two or three drops of oil (found in health-food stores everywhere) in a warm bath have an amazingly calming effect on children's nervous systems and works wonders.

Establishing New Habits

— **Dumping the day.** Invite your children, one at a time, to share anything they want to about their day without your "fixing" it, as a way of connecting heart-to-heart. In other words, your task is simply to listen to them and not try to change anything. When they're finished sharing their day (which may often consist of "dumping" their frustrations on you), ask them if they'd like you to do anything for them. Occasionally, they may answer yes and make a request, but often they'll say no, feeling satisfied with just being heard. Once they've unloaded the "bag of the day," you can then prepare for a visualization.

— **Inner journey.** Begin your visualization by dimming the lights and gently stroking your child's hair for a moment or two. Ask him to take a deep, cleansing breath, and then very slowly exhale. Have him do this two or three times, asking him to imagine relaxing a little more with each breath.

Next, ask your child to remember all the things about his day that may have taught him something new, something he may have never before discovered. Ask him to enjoy for just a moment what it felt like. Then give him a moment or two to reflect on it.

Quietly stroke his hair or back and ask him to focus on his breath, having him inhale and then gently exhale once again. After another 20 or 30 seconds, suggest to your child that he remember everything that might have upset him that day. Once he does so, ask him to imagine handing over all of his troubles to his guardian angel to work on while he sleeps.

Tell him that his angel will find solutions to his problems during the night, so he can let go and not worry about a thing. He can simply sleep and refresh himself. Then once again remind him to breathe deeply in and out, and to relax.

Finally, after another 10 or 20 seconds, name everything about your child that is good, loving, and true, such as:

- You are kind.
- You are intelligent.
- You are strong.
- You are intuitive.
- You are peaceful.
- You are loved, safe, and important to the world.

Finish by saying "I love you very much," and giving him a kiss. My children and I called this our "special good-night poem."

This evening ritual is very healing and has become a central part of our family life. Even though it only takes five or six minutes, it's so effective in helping parents connect with their children, guiding kids to relax and tune inward, and enabling everyone to feel supported by the Universe that it does wonders for the entire family. My own daughters got so much pleasure and nurturing from our special poem that I even tape-recorded it for them to listen to on evenings when I was away.

I've shared my ideas on doing a creative visualization, but only as a model for you to work with. Trust that your own words and images, which are particularly significant to you and your children, will flow easily and freely. Allow yourself to be creative and natural and the perfect visualization will come forth.

A final word about tuning inward and the need for quiet: Shut off the TV and insist on silence from time to time. We're so bombarded by noise that it becomes impossible to hear the soothing voice of our soul. When you go within as a means of accessing intuition, don't get hung up on the method, but just get clear on the concept. If you place value on taking a few moments in your day for contemplation and you encourage your children to do the same—not as an assignment but more as a gift to themselves—then their own awakened intuition will keep them coming back to it.

Establishing More New Habits

Encourage your children to:

- Sit quietly in a rocking chair and rock gently for 15 minutes.

- Float on an air mattress in a swimming pool with their eyes closed.

- Lie on the ground and watch clouds or count stars.

- Meditate on their favorite holiday before going to sleep.

- Imagine their guides.

- Listen to baroque music while lying on the floor with their eyes shut.

- Plant a garden.

- Work with clay or Play-Doh.

- Paint a picture.

- Learn to knit or build a model.

- Watch fish in an aquarium.

Reflections

- What are your children's favorite ways to "zone out" or "chill" (as my daughters now say)? What are yours?

- Do your kids have a special place to relax and tune inward?

- Do they need encouragement doing this? How can you help?

- Are you able to create quiet time for yourself? When and how? Have you benefited from the practice?

Reminders

Are you:

- Using your artistic talents?
- Reminding yourself to ask for help?
- Getting to know your guides?
- Remembering to create quiet time?

Chapter Fourteen

THE SOUL IS ETERNAL

A few years ago, my client Carla called me because she was very distressed about the recurring nightmares her daughter was having. Night after night, eight-year-old Ann woke up in a full sweat, screaming for her mom and refusing to go back to sleep unless Carla stayed with her until morning and kept the light on. Exhausted by these nocturnal disruptions and not knowing how to stop them, Carla asked for my advice.

"What exactly is she afraid of?" I asked.

"She's terrified that we're going to die or something. I'm not exactly sure why, because I keep telling her that we're all fine and not to think about it, but it isn't working. She's obsessed."

"Well, that's the problem," I said. "Your daughter is beginning to be aware of death and *needs* to talk to you about it for insight and reassurance. If you won't discuss it, then she feels that it must be far more terrible than she imagines. Her fears about dying take on a larger dimension than ever, scaring her even further."

"But I don't like focusing on that subject myself. It scares *me,* too," she responded. "I simply don't want to know about it! Every time I think about losing the girls or my husband—and especially my aging father—it's too upsetting."

"Well, Carla, it may very well be *your* feelings that are giving Ann nightmares," I told her. "Your own aversion to talking about death can actually be causing her to intuitively pick up on it and overreact. These anxieties are then manifested in her dream state. It would be so much healthier for you both to discuss the reality of dying openly and without fear."

I suggested to Carla that she see a spiritual counselor because it was time for her to get an education about death.

Acknowledge the Wheel of Life

My friend Lu Ann taught me the saying "What you don't own, will own you." The parts of life that are uncomfortable, like dying or loss, need to be acknowledged just as readily as the joyous ones. If you don't accept sadness, you won't readily experience happiness. If you don't prepare your children to deal with all phases of life, including both the delightful and the sorrowful, then when the wheel turns downward into death or other endings, they'll be overwhelmed and confused—or even worse, they may blame themselves for the losses they face. This is crippling to the soul.

Another client of mine, Rex, had many precognitive dreams as a child. He particularly remembers that when he was about ten years old, he had repeated ones about his grandmother dying. He told his mother and father about his dreams on several occasions, but rather than talking about them and what they might mean, they were dismissed as "nothing" and reassured him that his beloved Grandma was just fine. Unfortunately, she wasn't as well as everyone had assumed, and several weeks later, she died suddenly of a stroke.

Everyone in the family was in shock, especially Rex. Because his parents had continually disregarded his dreams, he actually felt as though he were somehow the cause of his grandmother's passing. He went into a terrible state of anxiety and depression, never talking to anyone about his belief that he "killed Gram" for fear of the repercussions. His feelings festered for years, always active in his unconscious mind.

It wasn't until he was an adult in therapy that he was able to discuss this childhood trauma and his guilt about it. With the help of an insightful and intuitive therapist, he came to understand that his dreams had been precognitive. He realized that his grandmother's soul was merely trying to tell him that she was preparing to leave the earthly plane, and perhaps was saying good-bye. It took many dialogues with his counselor and a lot of personal study about death and the soul for Rex to finally heal from that dark cloud of culpability that had hung over him all his life.

Shine a Bright Light on Death

I've seen so many clients who have inherited unhealthy, undeveloped, fearful ideas about life, death, and the nature of our eternal souls that have actually prevented them from taking the kinds of risks that naturally go along with reaching our full potential. After all, life is meant to be lived, and how can it be if every step is taken in an effort to avoid dying?

If you have a poor understanding or are extremely anxious about death, then perhaps this would be a good time to explore new spiritual thoughts about it. There are some fabulous books that may offer you comfort and insight. Two of my favorites are *Tuesdays with Morrie,* by Mitch Albom; and *A Year to Live,* by Stephen Levine. In fact, there are entire sections on death and dying in most bookstores that may open doors to different and more healing beliefs than those you now hold.

Another possibility is to meet with a spiritual counselor to discuss your fears until you come to some sense of peace. If you're actually facing the loss of a family member—through illness, for example—you may want to contact a hospice center. There you'll find profoundly caring individuals who will assist you during this transition with their loving and spiritually awakened guidance.

Often parents avoid talking about the subject of death with their children because they don't want to scare them. But as my teachers have shown me, denial isn't a form of protection. For example, my client Jenny told me that she'd recently lost her father to cancer. As hard as it was for her, she didn't want her five-year-old daughter, Shelly, who was very close to "Papa," to suffer through it as well. The entire time Papa was sick, she and her husband kept it from Shelly. As the grandfather became more visibly ill, they made up excuses for not visiting him, afraid that his appearance would upset the little girl.

Eventually Papa died, and after the funeral, Shelly was informed. She was shocked and devastated, as well as angry and hurt because she'd loved him and hadn't been able to comfort him or say good-bye in any way. Worse yet, she lost confidence that anyone else in her family was safe. Because Papa had disappeared from her life so suddenly, what would keep anyone else from doing the same? She went into such full-blown anxiety over the possibility of losing her parents that night after night, she cried herself to sleep or woke up with nightmares.

Shelly's problems got so out of hand that eventually Jenny had to seek psychological and spiritual help. In doing so, she learned that, all good intentions aside, she and her husband had definitely made a mistake in not allowing their daughter to experience Papa's illness and passing on as a natural part of her life. It still would have been difficult for her, but it would have been far better for her to have learned about death, as well as to have been able to say good-bye to her grandfather. Mother and daughter are both on the road to recovering from their grief with the help of their minister and a spiritual psychologist, and are now beginning to heal.

The surprising thing for Jenny in this experience was how much easier it was for Shelly to accept Papa's death once their minister explained to the little girl that it was his time to die and that, somehow, he'd completed his earthly pilgrimage and his spirit was returning to God. When Shelly understood that we all have a journey to make while we're here, and that passing over is a joyous completion of it, she calmed down because the cycle no longer seemed so chaotic. Although not fully comprehending the wheel of life and death, she nevertheless found solace in knowing that souls live on and that each one has a path. Even though it was huge learning curve for them all, Jenny and her family are now closer and more deeply comforted for having made the effort to grow in their understanding of their loss.

If you don't have a peaceful view of death, take steps to seek support and learning. Share what you discover and believe about it with your kids. My own spiritual tradition has taught me that although we have physical forms, we're more than just these: We're essentially *spiritual* beings. As such, we come to our earthly experience for the purpose of our soul's growth and creative expression. In order to do this, not only does our soul assume a body that provides a vehicle to achieve its goals, but it also chooses the family best suited to further assist in our spiritual development. When we complete our Divine plan for this life, the body—which is no longer needed—dies, and the soul returns to the realm of Spirit.

Because the soul's growth can be slow and difficult, it usually progresses very little during one lifetime. Therefore, once it has rested and reviewed the progress it made during the incarnation that just passed, it elects to return to the earthly plane, enter another body and family, and continue on to a new phase of spiritual development.

As my teacher Dr. Tully once put it to me: "Lifetimes are like classrooms, with death being recess." He also taught me that our physical selves coexist in harmony with all of nature, which we're as much a part of as the trees, plants, and animals.

The Spirit Lives On after Death

Understanding the cycles of the soul, I've come to see and share with my children how death is simply a natural aspect of the wheel of life. Perhaps your spiritual tradition is different from mine, and maybe you believe that the soul goes to heaven or simply dissolves into the heart of the Universe. No one living can be absolutely certain of the journey after it passes on—we can only intuit it. However, whatever beliefs feel true to you *are* right for you if they provide comfort, solace, and hope for the future.

Perhaps we can learn best from nature. Direct your children to notice its cycles; and point out the seasons of birth, life, death, and rebirth. Explain that we, too, are part of the ongoing process. Kids accept this very easily because it's natural.

Once my daughter Sonia asked, "Where do our spirits go after we die?"

I thought about it for a minute, then answered, "Our souls return to the Divine Source, to God, but our *spirits* live on in the hearts and memories of those who knew and loved us." And she was satisfied.

Many people distance their children from the subject of death due to their protective instincts, but no matter what we do, we can't shield our kids from it. It's only natural that we don't want them to be frightened or worried or to go through the pain of loss, but they do in fact have innate wisdom and the ability to adapt to life's cycles if we'll only trust and allow them to have an honest opportunity to do so. Insulating them from the reality of death cheats them out of the chance to perceive their place (and ours) in the larger scheme of things. In trying to avoid unpleasantness, many parents lose touch with their children's natural and intuitive openness, and underestimate how tuned in to the truth their kids really are—even when they're very young. Let me share an amusing anecdote to demonstrate how adaptable they can be.

Treat Death as Natural

When my niece, Nicole, was three years old, she had a favorite goldfish named Goldie that she'd won at her preschool fair. Goldie was her first pet, and Nicole developed a great attachment to her.

One morning about four weeks after Goldie's arrival, my sister Noelle dropped Nicole off at school and returned home to find the fish floating on her side, dead. Noelle panicked, thinking of how this would devastate Nicole. Just then the phone rang, and it was her father-in-law.

"My God, Noelle, what's the matter?" he asked, hearing the upset in her voice.

"Goldie's dead," Noelle answered with a sigh. "And I don't want to tell Nicole."

Knowing how fond of her fish Nicole was, and being an over-indulgent grandparent, he said, "Don't worry, Noelle, I'll be right over."

Thirty minutes later, Grandpa showed up with another goldfish, freshly purchased from the best pet shop in town, but it didn't look anything like Goldie, who'd been an ordinary specimen. *This* one was a Rolls-Royce of a goldfish.

"Thanks, Grandpa," Noelle said, "but Nicole will never go for this. She'll know right away."

"No, she won't," he insisted, plopping the new fish into the bowl. "Just act natural."

When she returned from school, Nicole flew out of the car and ran into the kitchen to see Goldie. Surprised to see her grandfather there, she gave him a kiss on the cheek and said, "Want to meet my fish, Grandpa?" She took him by the hand and led him over to the bowl. The grown-ups held their breath as Nicole peered in.

"Hey!" she exclaimed upon inspection. *"That's* not Goldie!" She turned and looked them both dead in the eyes. "What's going on?"

Noelle and Grandpa were busted.

"Nicole, honey, Goldie's dead. I found her floating on her side this morning," my sister told her.

"She is? Why?"

"I don't know," Noelle answered. "She must have been sick."

"What did you do with her?"

Noelle slowly opened a cupboard and pulled out a cup of water containing Goldie. Nicole stared silently at the fish for a full minute. "Poor Goldie," she murmured.

And that was it. No tears. No drama. Just "Poor Goldie." Then she surprised them by asking, "Should we flush her down the toilet?"

Her mother and grandfather sighed with relief and said, "That's a good idea, Nicole. Let's do it."

"Is that like heaven?" Nicole asked as she dumped Goldie into the toilet.

"For fish, it is," Noelle replied. And with the whoosh of water, they all waved good-bye to Goldie.

Noelle and Grandpa looked at each other in complete amazement and burst out laughing. Nicole had handled the loss gracefully. In fact, they both felt ridiculous about what they'd put themselves through. As silly as it was, it still showed Noelle that children *can* accept endings and that it's better not to assume anything less.

Talk Openly about Death When It Shows Up

Kids are very intuitive about death and dying, and are often the very first ones to notice or sense a transition of this sort coming. The worst thing parents can do is to try to shield their children from it, even if they believe they're protecting them from the pain that comes with loss. It's much better to teach them about it through dialogue and stories and by listening to their questions and offering real answers, not platitudes. Kids can sense when they're being brushed off and when they're being taken seriously. They also have a naturally intuitive way to deal with death on their own terms when it does show up—that is, if you're supportive and don't interfere with their ability to connect to their inner wisdom.

For example, several years ago, the father of one of Sonia's classmates was killed in a car accident. Kevin and his two siblings were guided through the loss of their dad by their spiritually aware mother in such a beautiful way that it touched me deeply. Every night for several months, their mom gathered them in the living room and invited them to talk about their father's death and how they felt about him being gone. Initially numb, all they could say was "Fine." But with her gentle prodding and persistence, they eventually opened up, and one by one shared their grief, anger, and sadness . . . and ultimately their acceptance of his passing. Even though it was devastating for all of them, the way their mother handled the situation prevented any of them from going through the process alone and helped them heal both individually and as a family.

Everyone needs to learn as young as possible that to love and live means to expect change and even loss and death. I'm not suggesting being morbid, but when such transitions do come into your life, be honest and fair enough to allow your kids to deal with them in their own way, sharing in their process rather than blocking it.

If your children have grandparents who are very old or sick, let your children know that Grandma or Grandpa may die soon. Talk to them honestly and ask if they want to visit. Don't force anything and be natural. Death is *not* something to fear—it's normal. The only bad thing about it is the attitude of people who forget that we're all spiritual beings, and not just physical bodies. When we remember that everyone is a soul traveler and that our spirits live on, our anxieties subside and we can then begin to accept death and heal from the loss it brings to us.

Two years ago, I spoke with a client named Leah, who'd adopted a four-year-old boy six months earlier. She was putting all her energy into helping Douglas adjust to his new home when, out of the blue, her dearly loved father died unexpectedly. Leah was devastated. Between the involvement with her new son and the loss of her dad, her emotions were pulled in every direction, and she was a wreck. She spaced out a lot, cried at times, and couldn't concentrate on anything. She was in great turmoil, wanting to create a good home for Doug while her own world had been shattered.

About two weeks after her father's death, Leah woke with a start to find her son standing next to her bed. "Mom, I just had a dream about Grandpa," he said. "He told me to tell you that he's okay and that he sent me here to be with you so that he could go home."

"What?" she asked groggily, coming out of a deep sleep. "What was that?"

"I dreamed that Grandpa came to see me and said he's fine. He told me to take care of you," Douglas repeated, smiling. It was an unexpected gift, and because of it, she immediately began to heal.

In awakening our children's intuitive hearts, we need to allow for all of their concerns, feelings, dreams, precognition, and intuition. These will inevitably involve both life and death transitions, and we must provide our kids with a spiritually healthy framework to help them respond easily. That way, they can let themselves fully experience all of life's Divine gifts.

Be open to all of your children's intuitive musings. When they speak of death, share with them what you feel. And when they dream about it, let them talk out their fears. If someone in your family is dying, discuss it openly. Visit that person with your kids if possible, and urge them to ask questions and express their feelings. Reassure them and let them know that death is natural and never their fault, and that the spirit in all of us lives on and remains in our hearts.

The more a family can identify with one another as spiritual beings instead of as mere physical selves, the more everyone will be able to relate intuitively to all that's possible and present in each soul—and the less frightening death will become. This is the basis of a healthy intuition . . . knowing that there's so much more to who we are than simply the bodies we inhabit. Your children will sense this naturally and just need to have it affirmed by you.

Establishing New Habits:
Tools for Discovering the Eternal Soul

— **Look back.** Together with your children, explore your forebears on both sides of the family. If possible, look at photographs of grandmothers, grandfathers, and great-grandparents. Talk about their lives and what they contributed to their descendants that affects you today.

— **Create a tree of life.** Build a family tree on a piece of poster board, using photos if they're available. If they aren't, ask your kids to draw their ancestors.

— **Realize that it's only natural.** Take a walk outdoors in nature. Search the ground for living things in various stages of decay and rebirth, such as an acorn that can grow into a tree. Help your children notice the wheel of life, and point out to them in as many ways as possible how we're all connected to the earth and to one another.

— **Demonstrate that we're all one.** As you sit down to dinner, have your kids think about where their food comes from. Show them how it gives them energy and provides them with their life force. Ask them to bless the nourishment that supports their lives and to in turn share their creative power with the world.

— **Explore the past and future.** Take your children on a walking tour of a graveyard and discover who has lived and died. Imagine who these people might have been and invent tales about their lives. Invite the spirits of the dead to tell you their stories and to share with you their contributions to the earth. Picture their descendants and what they might be like today. Then pretend that these souls have each come back into a body and have new lives. What would they be like? Enjoy this exercise and let your imaginations run wild!

— **Be there.** Visit a relative or friend who's aging or sick. Don't be afraid to ask them what it's like to be in their place and how you can best help them during this time.

It's also helpful to:

- Encourage your children to talk to their dead relatives and forebears in their hearts and to ask them for support and love in their lives today.

- Talk about your family's various ancestors and their particular strengths and gifts.

- Ask your children which of these individuals may be best suited to assist them with the challenges of life. For example, Grandpa the gardener may help your child with patience, Grandma the champion housekeeper could pitch in with organization, Aunt Millie the artist could provide inspiration, and so forth.

- Discuss death and the afterlife with your children and let them know that even though the forms life takes change, the spirit in all of us lives on forever.

Reflections

- Who's your favorite ancestor? Who are your children's?

- Imagine the future generations of your family and invent stories about who they are and what they might be like.

- Invite your kids to notice and share as many examples of the wheel of life as possible. Also give them some of your own.

- Write about your personal connection with your kids—past and future. Let your spirit guide you in this exercise.

- Have you talked with your children about death? How do they feel about it?

- Is anyone in your family sick, aging, or dying? How do you feel about this?

- Do you openly speak about loved ones who have passed away?

- Have you allowed the spirits of the deceased to continue contributing to your lives?

Reminders

Are you:

- Remembering to ask for help?
- Getting to know your guides?
- Reminding yourself to create quiet time?
- Aware of your eternal nature?

Epilogue

KINDRED SPIRITS
IN THE WHEEL OF LIFE

In my childhood, being in touch with the unseen world wasn't only a family affair—it was a community one. In addition to having the influence of my mother and her friends, I grew up in a primarily Hispanic Catholic area where there was much emphasis placed on soul and Spirit. We talked to our guardian angels, prayed to our patron saints and asked them for protection, and implored and received the love and guidance of the Holy Mother. We danced with Spirit as a matter of course.

By the time I was 12, I knew several families like mine, who communicated as comfortably on an intuitive level as they did on the phone. My world was never heady or intellectual—it was far more sensual and spiritual . . . and it wasn't isolated.

One of the greatest problems I see in my work with clients is that so many people have overvalued their heads and lost touch with their hearts. Our cerebral side is wonderful for informing us about the visible world, but can lose its way on the unseen plane—and appearances can be very deceiving indeed. To our eyes, we seem separate and different from one another; to our intellects, superior or inferior; and to our logic, threatened and even endangered by each other. And so we withdraw, put up defenses, and become fearful and suspicious. We lose our confidence, which dims our awareness, leading us into an ever more isolated and spiritually bankrupt state.

The unseen world, on the other hand, is heart based. It reveals the hidden truth behind appearances and shows us our connection to and need for one another. It opens our hearts and then our hands, moving us to reach out and touch each other. This is a truer realm and is where cooperation and creativity can thrive, making it safer than the place our intellectual voices have created.

Perhaps because my mother lost contact with her entire family during the war, she was very committed to creating a new one, which extended beyond our nucleus. She "adopted" our friends and called each of the children on the block "one of my kids." Our door was open to everyone; and our conversations about love, life, adventures, and vibes traveled far beyond our own family members. It was normal to find many kids from other homes hanging around our kitchen table every day. When I was a teenager, ours was the house other young people came to.

The spiritual community of intuitive support afforded me a rich and diverse vein of gold in which to explore and discover the world of the soul with friends. All these avenues of six-sensory play were like another piece of a complex quilt that warmly embraced my inner discoveries, keeping me safe, protected, and forever burning with a feverish desire to know more.

I fully believe that growing up in such a diverse spiritual culture has greatly aided my ability to freely access my own intuitive world, and it's a legacy I continue to pass along to my children. I've invited my girls to get to know and befriend people of all ages as part of their circle of wise elders. My friends are their friends as well, and vice versa.

As parents, we may have blind spots or weaknesses that other members of our spiritual family can help us recognize and overcome. Because our kids understand that we have our foibles, they first look to us, and then *beyond* us for support and guidance—to other creative hearts and ultimately to God. In my community, we all speak the same language of spirit. Together we help and support one another in profound and diverse ways. It's the part of my life I love and cherish the most.

Above all, be yourself. No matter what, never forget that the children you have in your life chose *you* to guide them. Take whatever suggestions from this book feel right to you and ignore the ones that don't. You're naturally the best and most qualified person in the world to intuitively know what's right and true for you and your kids.

Take hold of your own innate, organic wisdom. Leave your fears behind and center your full awareness on your heart. Seek counsel and guidance whenever you deem it necessary for your children, but always put this to the vibe test. And remember: Don't surrender your natural intuition—even in the face of the most daunting authority.

Reclaiming your sixth sense and restoring it to its rightful place of honor in your kids' lives will give them an invaluable gift, making them aware of the wonder in the world. It will open their eyes and ears to the glory and delight of creativity, arm them with confidence, provide added insurance for protection, and help them connect to their real purpose and to those with whom they share their days. It will assure them of their natural place in the wheel of life and aid them in overcoming the fear of death. And above all, it will give them the right to live in peace without being afraid, and to have the full experience of discovering who they really are. This is the natural way and as it should be.

It's my hope that you—and they—will live deeply empowered by their intuitive gifts ever after.

May God bless you, your children, and your home.

— *All my love,*
Sonia

About the Author

Sonia Choquette is a world-renowned author, storyteller, vibrational healer, and six-sensory spiritual teacher in international demand for her guidance, wisdom, and capacity to heal the soul. She's the author of several best-selling books, including *Ask Your Guides, Trust Your Vibes, Soul Lessons and Soul Purpose;* and numerous audio programs and card decks. Sonia was educated at the University of Denver and the Sorbonne in Paris, and holds a Ph.D. in metaphysics from the American Institute of Holistic Theology. She resides with her family in Chicago.

Website: **www.soniachoquette.com**

Notes

Notes

Notes

Notes

Notes

Notes

Notes

Notes

Notes

Notes

HAY HOUSE TITLES OF RELATED INTEREST

THE ASTONISHING POWER OF EMOTIONS:
Let Your Feelings Be Your Guide, by Esther and Jerry Hicks
(The Teachings of Abraham™)

FOUR ACTS OF PERSONAL POWER: *How to Heal Your Past
and Create a Positive Future,* by Denise Linn

YOUR SOUL'S COMPASS: *What Is Spiritual Guidance?*
by Joan Z. Borysenko, Ph.D., and Gordon Franklin Dveirin, Ed.D.

HEALING YOUR FAMILY HISTORY: *5 Steps to Break Free
of Destructive Patterns,* by Rebecca Linder Hintze

THE TIMES OF OUR LIVES: *Extraordinary True Stories
of Synchronicity, Destiny, Meaning, and Purpose,*
by Louise L. Hay and Friends

TRANSFORMING FATE INTO DESTINY:
A New Dialogue with Your Soul, by Robert Ohotto
(available March 2008)

All of the above are available at your local bookstore,
or may be ordered by contacting Hay House (see next page).

We hope you enjoyed this Hay House Hay Housebook.
If you'd like to receive a free catalog featuring additional
Hay House books and products, or if you'd like information
about the Hay Foundation, please contact:

Hay House, Inc.
P.O. Box 5100
Carlsbad, CA 92018-5100

(760) 431-7695 or (800) 654-5126
(760) 431-6948 (fax) or (800) 650-5115 (fax)
www.hayhouse.com® • www.hayfoundation.org

Published and distributed in Australia by: Hay House Australia Pty. Ltd.,
18/36 Ralph St., Alexandria NSW 2015 *Phone:* 612-9669-4299
Fax: 612-9669-4144 • www.hayhouse.com.au

Published and distributed in the United Kingdom by: Hay House UK, Ltd.,
292B Kensal Rd., London W10 5BE • *Phone:* 44-20-8962-1230
Fax: 44-20-8962-1239 • www.hayhouse.co.uk

Published and distributed in the Republic of South Africa by:
Hay House SA (Pty), Ltd., P.O. Box 990, Witkoppen 2068
Phone/Fax: 27-11-467-8904 • orders@psdprom.co.za
www.hayhouse.co.za

Published in India by: Hay House Publishers India, Muskaan Complex,
Plot No. 3, B-2, Vasant Kunj, New Delhi 110 070 • *Phone:* 91-11-4176-1620
Fax: 91-11-4176-1630 • www.hayhouse.co.in

Distributed in Canada by: Raincoast, 9050 Shaughnessy St.,
Vancouver, B.C. V6P 6E5 • *Phone:* (604) 323-7100
Fax: (604) 323-2600 • www.raincoast.com

Tune in to **HayHouseRadio.com®** for the best in
inspirational talk radio featuring top Hay House authors!
And, sign up via the Hay House USA Website to receive the
Hay House online newsletter and stay informed about what's
going on with your favorite authors. You'll receive bimonthly
announcements about Discounts and Offers, Special Events,
Product Highlights, Free Excerpts, Giveaways, and more!
www.hayhouse.com®